Reading Links

2

Andrew E. Bennett

NAN'UN-DO

Reading Links 2

Written and designed by: Andrew E. Bennett

Reading Links 2
Image Credits

Shutterstock: pp. 8, 16, 18, 20, 36, 44, 48, 56, 60, 64, 72, 76, 78, 80, 86 (© Shutterstock);
Gui Yu: p. 12 (© Andrew E. Bennett);
Corel Gallery: p. 14 (right) (© Corel);
Hemera: pp. 14 (left), 32, 66 (top, second from top, third from top), 84 (© Hemera);
iStock Photos: pp. 22, 24, 28, 40, 68 (© iStock Photos);
A-Tai: p. 38 (© Andrew E. Bennett);
Corel: p. 52 (© Corel);
Q Vision: p. 54 (© Q Vision);
EnA: p. 66 (bottom) (© EnA Digital Arts);
Sun Zi Xing & Chen Yan Min: p. 70 (© Andrew E. Bennett);
Idea Design Center: p. 74 (© Idea Design Center)

Contents

Download Audio

音声ファイル
無料 DL
のご案内

このテキストの音声を無料で視聴（ストリーミング）・ダウンロードできます。自習用音声としてご活用ください。
以下のサイトにアクセスしてテキスト番号で検索してください。

https://nanun-do.com　テキスト番号［**512092**］

※ 無線 LAN（WiFi）に接続してのご利用を推奨いたします。

※ 音声ダウンロードは Zip ファイルでの提供になります。
お使いの機器によっては別途ソフトウェア（アプリケーション）の導入が必要となります。

Read by

Rachel Walzer
Chris Koprowski

※ Reading Links 2 音声ダウンロードページは
以下の QR コードからもご利用になれます。

Introduction

Reading Links is a comprehensive series designed for lower-level students. Each book includes 20 units centered on high-interest topics such as the arts, careers, entertainment, the environment, and many others.

Reading passages and exercises use carefully controlled vocabulary and grammar to facilitate comprehension. Critical thinking and active student engagement are also encouraged. Unit after unit, students' reading, vocabulary, grammar, listening, and speaking skills are strengthened.

Following is an explanation of the unit components:

The general topic is given next to the unit number.

Units are divided into two parts covering different aspects of the topic. Part 1 starts with a story or article. In *Reading Links 2*, these passages are between 75-100 words long. The track number next to the headphones icon corresponds to the downloadable audio recording of the passage.

This vocabulary building exercise contains four target words or phrases selected from the reading passage. They are chosen for their frequency and usefulness. To build fluency further, students can be asked to write their own sentences using the target words.

1 Weather

Part 1: Making Rain

Read the following article. Track 2

People in cities use a lot of water – for cooking, washing, drinking, and so on. Rain is the main source of new water. Unfortunately, it doesn't always rain enough. That can be a big problem for cities.

Sometimes, we can help make it rain. To do this, a special airplane flies up to the clouds. Then, it releases some chemicals. These chemicals cause clouds to make rain. The process is called "seeding clouds." It brings water to thirsty cities.

Vocabulary Check Write the correct word in each blank.

thirsty	unfortunately	fly	cause

1. Typhoons ____________ big problems for areas near the ocean.
2. The dog looks ____________. I'll give it something to drink.
3. ____________, I can't go with you to the party.
4. Many birds ____________ south in the winter.

8

Reading Check Choose the best answer.

1. ( ) What does the article say about rain?
   A: We don't understand why it rains.
   B: Rain water is mostly used for drinking.
   C: Unfortunately, it usually rains too much.
   D: It is the main way cities get water.
2. ( ) Without enough rain, ___________.
   A: people do a lot of cooking
   B: businesses use more water
   C: stores must close their doors
   D: cities have problems
3. ( ) What is "seeding clouds"?
   A: a kind of cloud
   B: a way to make it rain
   C: a chemical
   D: a special airplane
4. ( ) What happens first?
   A: The clouds are seeded by chemicals.
   B: It starts to rain heavily.
   C: Chemicals are loaded onto an airplane.
   D: An airplane flies up high.

Grammar Check Complete each sentence with *do*, *doesn't*, or *don't*.

Ex: No, my sister *doesn't* speak French.

1. Let me check. Yes, I __________ have enough money.
2. She __________ want to go ice skating.
3. The kids sure __________ love ice cream. They always ask for it.
4. No, they __________ enjoy living next to the highway.

9

This reading comprehension exercise includes detail, analysis, and vocabulary questions. Some questions go beneath the surface, encouraging students to consider the material more deeply and employ critical thinking skills.

Each grammar check covers an important language structure such as pronouns, word forms, verb tenses, prepositions, and so on. There are also several word order exercises in which students rearrange words to make a complete sentence.

Part 2 opens with a unique element of *Reading Links*: a visual reading component. It is included because in today's world, literacy extends beyond the ability to read passages of text. It means being able to read maps, graphs, tables, charts, schedules, dialogues, and so on.

In *Reading Links*, these components are presented in simplified, yet authentic English to provide students an opportunity to practice and improve these critical 21st century skills.

Part 2: Rainfall and Travel Plans

Read the following information.

Average Monthly Rainfall in Mexico City

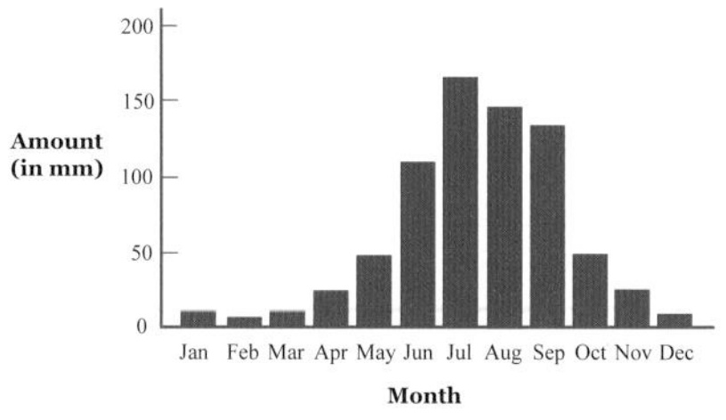

Jill and Simon are planning a trip to Mexico City. They prefer dry weather. Also, they don't like traveling in the winter. Simon cannot travel in October. He has important work to do back home.

True or False Circle true (T) or false (F).

1. (T/F) February is the month with the most rainfall.
2. (T/F) In May, Mexico City receives about 50 mm of rainfall.
3. (T/F) The rainfall is below 150 mm every month.
4. (T/F) July is the best month for Jill and Simon's trip.

10

This basic true and false exercise checks students' understanding of the material. Teachers are encouraged to go further and base classroom activities on the visual reading components through role plays, student-generated materials and presentations, etc.

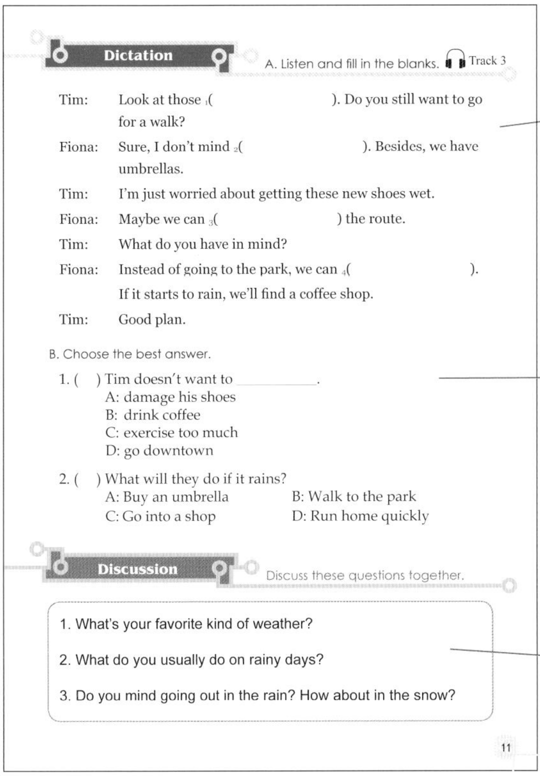

Dictation

A. Listen and fill in the blanks. Track 3

Tim: Look at those 1(   ). Do you still want to go for a walk?

Fiona: Sure, I don't mind 2(   ). Besides, we have umbrellas.

Tim: I'm just worried about getting these new shoes wet.

Fiona: Maybe we can 3(   ) the route.

Tim: What do you have in mind?

Fiona: Instead of going to the park, we can 4(   ). If it starts to rain, we'll find a coffee shop.

Tim: Good plan.

B. Choose the best answer.

1. (   ) Tim doesn't want to ________.
   A: damage his shoes
   B: drink coffee
   C: exercise too much
   D: go downtown

2. (   ) What will they do if it rains?
   A: Buy an umbrella
   B: Walk to the park
   C: Go into a shop
   D: Run home quickly

Discussion

Discuss these questions together.

1. What's your favorite kind of weather?
2. What do you usually do on rainy days?
3. Do you mind going out in the rain? How about in the snow?

11

This dialogue is related to the unit's general topic. The track number next to the headphones icon corresponds to the downloadable audio recording of the dialogue. Students should listen to the audio recording and fill in the blanks. As a fluency building exercise, students can then pair up and take turns reading each character's lines.

The dialogue is followed by a comprehension exercise.

Finally, there is a series of discussion questions related to Part 1 and Part 2 of the unit. Students may ask each other questions in pairs, or the class can answer the questions together. Students are encouraged to go beyond "yes/no" answers and provide examples and details from their own lives, as well as reasons for their points of view.

Additional materials for *Reading Links 2* are available. They include downloadable MP3 files of the audio recordings, which make it easy for students to listen to the recordings on their computer, phone, or other device.

The book's teacher's manual includes the full listening transcript, answer key, and other resources.

Materials to assist with online classes are also available from Nan'un-do.

I hope *Reading Links 2* helps build students' English skills while boosting everyone's interest and confidence in an enjoyable way.

Thank you very much, and best wishes for an outstanding class!

Andrew E. Bennett

1 Weather

Part 1: Making Rain

Read the following article. Track 2

People in cities use a lot of water – for cooking, washing, drinking, and so on. Rain is the main source of new water. Unfortunately, it doesn't always rain enough. That can be a big problem for cities.

Sometimes, we can help make it rain. To do this, a special airplane flies up to the clouds. Then, it releases some chemicals. These chemicals cause clouds to make rain. The process is called "seeding clouds." It brings water to thirsty cities.

Vocabulary Check

Write the correct word in each blank.

thirsty	unfortunately	fly	cause

1. Typhoons ____________ big problems for areas near the ocean.
2. The dog looks ____________. I'll give it something to drink.
3. ____________, I can't go with you to the party.
4. Many birds ____________ south in the winter.

Reading Check

Choose the best answer.

1. (   ) What does the article say about rain?
   A: We don't understand why it rains.
   B: Rain water is mostly used for drinking.
   C: Unfortunately, it usually rains too much.
   D: It is the main way cities get water.

2. (   ) Without enough rain, ________.
   A: people do a lot of cooking
   B: businesses use more water
   C: stores must close their doors
   D: cities have problems

3. (   ) What is "seeding clouds"?
   A: a kind of cloud
   B: a way to make it rain
   C: a chemical
   D: a special airplane

4. (   ) What happens first?
   A: The clouds are seeded by chemicals.
   B: It starts to rain heavily.
   C: Chemicals are loaded onto an airplane.
   D: An airplane flies up high.

Grammar Check

Complete each sentence with *do*, *doesn't*, or *don't*.

Ex: No, my sister *doesn't* speak French.

1. Let me check. Yes, I ________ have enough money.

2. She ________ want to go ice skating.

3. The kids sure ________ love ice cream. They always ask for it.

4. No, they ________ enjoy living next to the highway.

Part 2: Rainfall and Travel Plans

Read the following information.

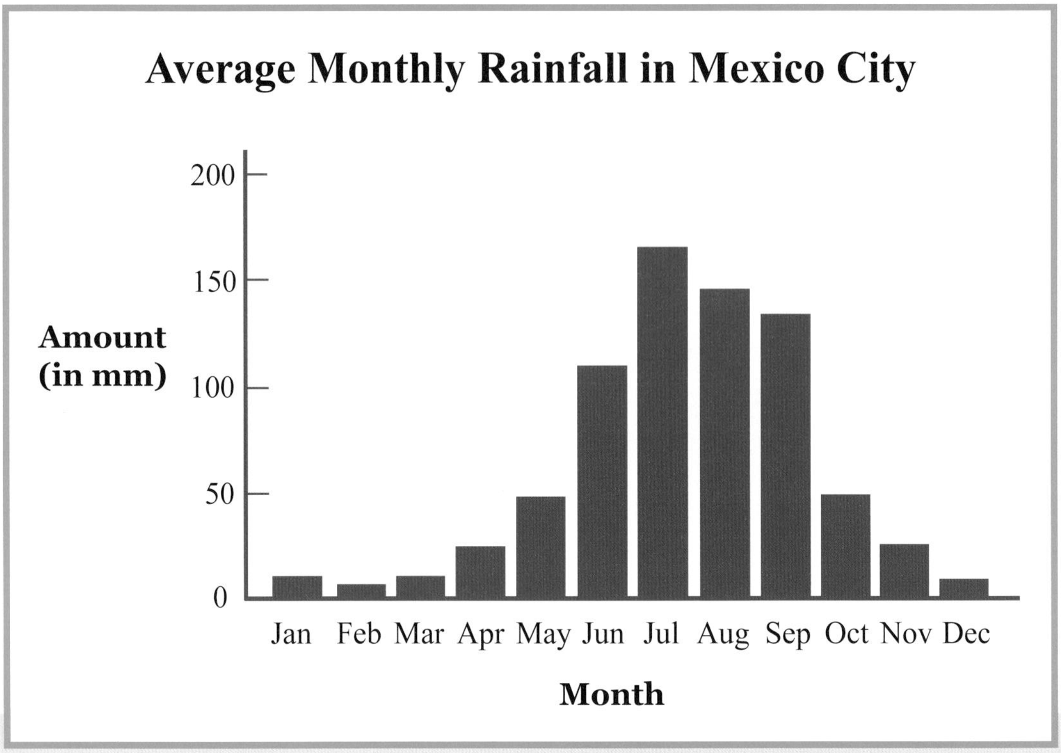

Jill and Simon are planning a trip to Mexico City. They prefer dry weather. Also, they don't like traveling in the winter. Simon cannot travel in October. He has important work to do back home.

True or False

Circle true (T) or false (F).

1. (T/F) February is the month with the most rainfall.
2. (T/F) In May, Mexico City receives about 50 mm of rainfall.
3. (T/F) The rainfall is below 150 mm every month.
4. (T/F) July is the best month for Jill and Simon's trip.

Dictation

A. Listen and fill in the blanks. Track 3

Tim: Look at those $_{1}$( ). Do you still want to go for a walk?

Fiona: Sure, I don't mind $_{2}$( ). Besides, we have umbrellas.

Tim: I'm just worried about getting these new shoes wet.

Fiona: Maybe we can $_{3}$( ) the route.

Tim: What do you have in mind?

Fiona: Instead of going to the park, we can $_{4}$( ). If it starts to rain, we'll find a coffee shop.

Tim: Good plan.

B. Choose the best answer.

1. ( ) Tim doesn't want to ____________.
   A: damage his shoes
   B: drink coffee
   C: exercise too much
   D: go downtown

2. ( ) What will they do if it rains?
   A: Buy an umbrella
   B: Walk to the park
   C: Go into a shop
   D: Run home quickly

Discussion

Discuss these questions together.

1. What's your favorite kind of weather?
2. What do you usually do on rainy days?
3. Do you mind going out in the rain? How about in the snow?

2 The Internet

Part 1: Online Gaming

Read the following article. Track 4

Before the Internet, people usually played computer games at home, either alone or with friends. Going online is now fast and affordable, and computer gaming is changing. With a computer, cell phone, or other device, people everywhere can play together.

There are many kinds of online games. Some are for playing sports, chess, and other traditional games. Others are "role-playing" games. In these games, each player becomes a character in an online world. Online gaming is a fast-growing business with an exciting future. Plus, it's a lot of fun!

Vocabulary Check

Write the correct word in each blank.

alone	changes	traditional	world

1. Everything in today's cities __________ so quickly.

2. The __________ is big. But it's easy to fly from place to place.

3. I don't like being __________. I prefer spending time with friends.

4. This __________ holiday song is heard everywhere in December.

Reading Check

Choose the best answer.

1. ( ) To play online games, people need ________.
   A: an expensive computer
   B: a fast-growing and successful business
   C: a lot of friends at home
   D: a computer or device like a cell phone

2. ( ) According to the article, the Internet is ________.
   A: not affordable
   B: only fast on some cell phones
   C: cheap, but slow
   D: changing how we play games

3. ( ) What kind of computer game is not discussed?
   A: Role-playing games
   B: Strategy games
   C: Traditional games
   D: Sports games

4. ( ) Which of the following is true?
   A: Every computer is connected to the Internet.
   B: The earliest computers could play games online.
   C: In some online games, players become characters.
   D: The online gaming business is growing slowly.

Grammar Check

Write the past tense form of each verb.

Ex: Derek *showed* (show) me his new gaming system.

1. Yesterday, we ________ (play) soccer all day.

2. I ________ (send) a message to Sheila this morning.

3. Tina ________ (buy) a dress in Harajuku.

4. Going to the aquarium ________ (be) so much fun!

Look at the following website.

www.fastnews.com

Main sections
- Nation
- World
- Business
- Sports
- Entertainment

Other sections
- Free e-mail
- Live video
- Reader polls

Top Stories

“Red” is a hero.

Nation
Pet dog saves man’s life

World
Germany’s new leader

Business
Sony’s profits rise 20%

Sports
Two weeks until the World Cup starts

Entertainment
The new James Bond movie

Website search go

Internet search go

Advertisement

JAKE'S PIZZA
Order online or on our app!

True or False

Circle true (T) or false (F).

1. (T/F) The website has a special section about cats.
2. (T/F) Website visitors can watch a live video feed.
3. (T/F) Fastnews.com does not have games on the website.
4. (T/F) The advertisement is at the top of the page.

Dictation

A. Listen and fill in the blanks. Track 5

Tracy: Fantasy Rush is 1(   )!

Leo: I just started playing yesterday. I can't believe it's free. How does the website make money?

Tracy: They sell you things 2(   ). You can buy a horse and magic rings – stuff like that.

Leo: Oh, I see. I'm still on the first level. I just like 3(   ) and looking at things.

Tracy: You'll be fine for a while. On the higher levels, it helps to have a flying horse.

Leo: Thanks, that's 4(   ).

B. Choose the best answer.

1. (   ) Tracy has probably ________.
   A: played the game less than Leo
   B: tried some of the game's higher levels
   C: never bought something in the game
   D: sold some magic rings to Leo

2. (   ) What does Leo enjoy doing in Fantasy Rush?
   A: Looking at the game world
   B: Riding a flying horse
   C: Buying and selling things
   D: Meeting other players

Discussion

Discuss these questions together.

1. Do you play any online games? If so, which ones?
2. Do you have any favorite websites?
3. How about mobile apps? Do you have any favorites?

Part 1: Dolphins

Read the following article. Track 6

Dolphins live in the world's oceans. There are more than 30 species of these beautiful animals. Some live in small groups with just a few members. Others live in large groups of 10,000 dolphins or more.

Dolphins are interesting animals. They use loud squeaking noises to communicate with each other. Plus, they swim very fast – up to 40 kilometers per hour. Dolphins also enjoy being with people. They often swim alongside boats. There are even stories of dolphins saving swimmers in trouble.

Vocabulary Check

Write the correct word in each blank.

group	communicate	save	trouble

1. Doctors ______________ lives every day.

2. I use a phone app to ______________ with far-away friends.

3. A ______________ of rabbits live in the park.

4. This bike gives me so much ______________. I've fixed it three times.

Reading Check

Choose the best answer.

1. (   ) Dolphin groups ____________.
   A: are always small
   B: cannot have more than 1,000 members
   C: sometimes include very few dolphins
   D: are usually large

2. (   ) How do dolphins communicate?
   A: By swimming quickly
   B: By finding a large group
   C: By talking to people
   D: By making loud noises

3. (   ) What is a "member"?
   A: a species of dolphin   B: a part of a group
   C: a kind of animal   D: a number or size

4. (   ) Dolphins ____________ people.
   A: sometimes help
   B: cause trouble for
   C: stay away from
   D: are a danger to

Grammar Check

Write the correct word in each blank.

Ex: One of the ___*windows*___ **is open.**
(window / windows)

1. She is the leader of this ____________.
   (group/groups)

2. The repair job will require more ____________ than the last one.
   (work/works)

3. Mindy is one of my good ____________.
   (friend/friends)

4. The zoo has more than 150 ____________.
   (animal/animals)

Part 2: Amazing Sea Animals

Read the following information.

Cetaceans are sea mammals. The group includes dolphins, porpoises, and whales. Here are some interesting facts about them.

Dolphins	The squeaking noises of dolphins form an actual language. This language differs from group to group.
	When speaking, dolphins use names for each other.
	Some orcas (a type of dolphin) are more than 10 meters long.

Porpoises	There are six different porpoise species.
	The fastest porpoises can swim 30 km/hr.
	Porpoises have up to 120 teeth. They hunt for fish and other sea creatures.

Whales	Blue whales are the world's largest animals. They weigh up to 150 tons.
	Many whales sing, and their songs can last 30 minutes.
	Whales sleep on the water's surface.

True or False

Circle true (T) or false (F).

1. (T / F) Some porpoises are larger than blue whales.
2. (T / F) The language of dolphins is the same for every group.
3. (T / F) Whale songs may last half an hour.
4. (T / F) Dolphins call each other by their names.

Dictation

A. Listen and fill in the blanks. Track 7

Ken: Look at that beautiful, $_{1}$( ).

Laura: It's a perfect day for swimming.

Ken: Or whale watching. Do you still have that $_{2}$( ) pamphlet?

Laura: I do. It says the boat $_{3}$( ) at 10:30. It goes out to an area with dolphins, whales, and sea lions.

Ken: I'd be happy seeing any of them in the ocean. Anyway, it's 8:30 now. Should we give it a try?

Laura: Let's do it. We can drive to the harbor $_{4}$( ).

B. Choose the best answer.

1. ( ) Ken had the idea to ____________.
   A: make breakfast B: call the boating company
   C: see whales in the ocean D: go swimming

2. ( ) What do we learn about the boat ride?
   A: People must be on the boat by 8:30.
   B: You might see three kinds of animals.
   C: They give everyone food and drinks.
   D: The boat ride lasts about two hours.

Discussion

Discuss these questions together.

1. Do you like going to the beach? How about taking boat rides?
2. Have you ever seen a dolphin or whale up close? If so, where was it?
3. Do you have any pets? If so, what kind? If not, would you like to have pets one day?

4 Friends

Part 1: The Last Day of the Last Class

Read the following story. Track 8

Tammy, Linda, and Jennifer were best friends. They attended the same junior high school, senior high school, and even university together. The three friends had a nice custom. Every year, after the last day of class, they took some photographs together.

As the saying goes, all good things must come to an end. The last day of their last year of university finally arrived. The three friends went to their favorite mall. They took several pictures using a photo machine. It was the final year of their custom, so they were a little sad. But they were happy to have so many good memories.

Vocabulary Check

Write the correct word in each blank.

attend	memories	university	final

1. I have nice ____________ of living in England.

2. What time does the ____________ train leave the station?

3. I hope you can ____________ the meeting.

4. Do you plan to go to a(n) ____________ near your house?

Reading Check

Choose the best answer.

1. (   ) When did the friends take photos together?
   A: At the end of each school year
   B: During winter vacation
   C: Every day after class
   D: Three times a year

2. (   ) What was special about the friends' trip to the mall?
   A: It was their first time taking photos together.
   B: The mall had discounted prices that day.
   C: The friends were happier than ever.
   D: The friends knew their custom was ending.

3. (   ) "...all good things must come to an end." What does that mean?
   A: Nothing lasts forever.
   B: Only the best things in life have good endings.
   C: All things start on time.
   D: When you say something, make sure it's right.

4. (   ) Which of the following is true?
   A: The three friends first met each other in university.
   B: During high school, the friends didn't follow their custom.
   C: The friends took more than one photograph at the mall.
   D: The father of one of the friends owned a camera store.

Grammar Check

Match the beginning and ending of each sentence.

Ex: I'm tired,	so we'd better hurry up.
1. We're late,	so I have to study a lot.
2. He needs more money,	so I'm going to sleep.
3. The class is hard,	so they won't go for a bike ride.
4. They expect it to rain,	so he's looking for a new job.

Part 2: New Friends

Read the following conversation.

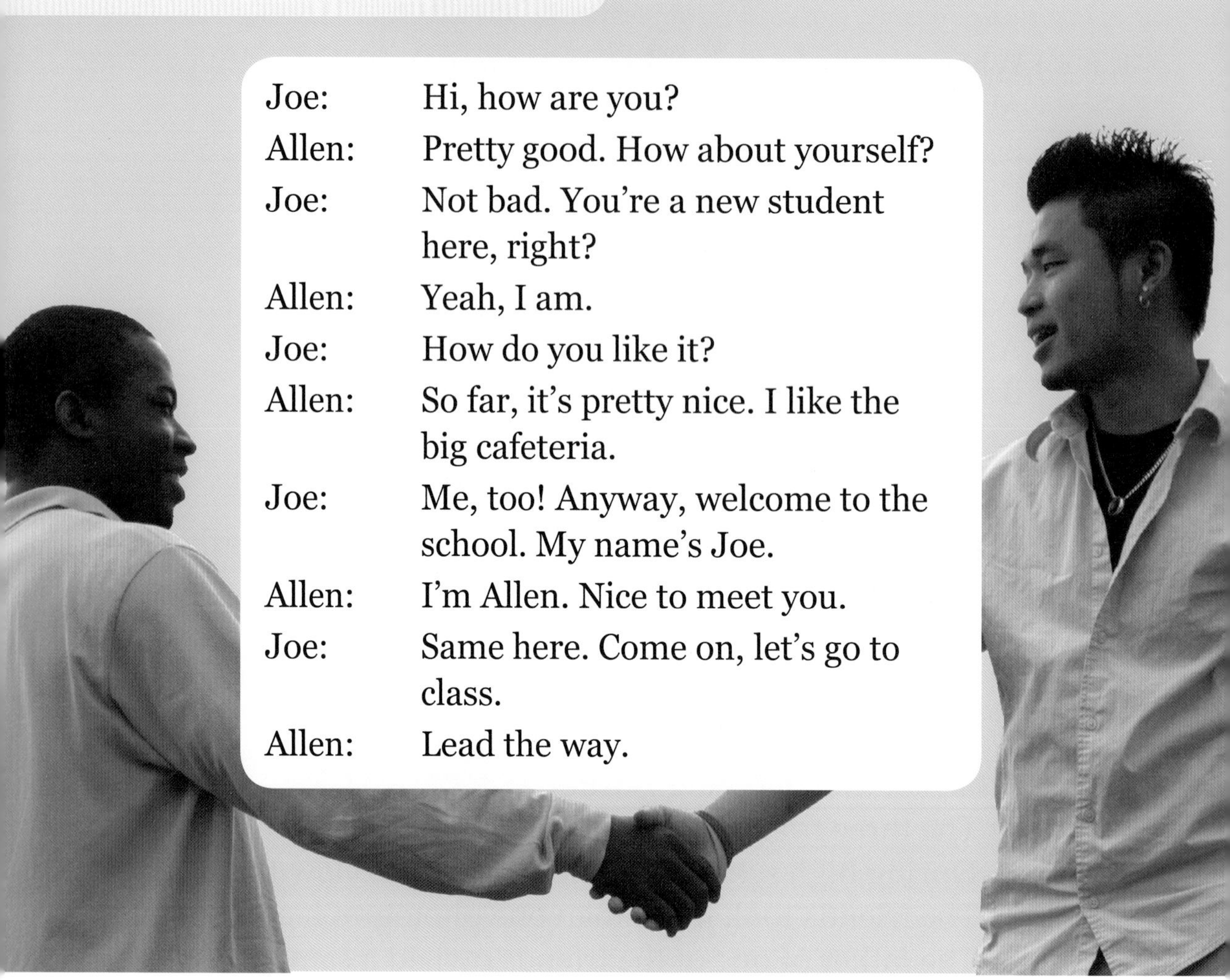

Joe:	Hi, how are you?
Allen:	Pretty good. How about yourself?
Joe:	Not bad. You're a new student here, right?
Allen:	Yeah, I am.
Joe:	How do you like it?
Allen:	So far, it's pretty nice. I like the big cafeteria.
Joe:	Me, too! Anyway, welcome to the school. My name's Joe.
Allen:	I'm Allen. Nice to meet you.
Joe:	Same here. Come on, let's go to class.
Allen:	Lead the way.

True or False

Circle true (T) or false (F).

1. (T/F) Allen and Joe are classmates.

2. (T/F) Joe just started attending the school.

3. (T/F) Joe says, "Not bad." He means he's doing fine.

4. (T/F) Allen likes the school's cafeteria.

Dictation

A. Listen and fill in the blanks. Track 9

Daniel:	How are your 1( ) going?
Aya:	Really well. They're all interesting so far. Also, the workload isn't heavy.
Daniel:	That's a big change from 2( ), right?
Aya:	I'll say. With my part-time job, I barely had any free time.
Daniel:	I remember. Are you still working at the 3( )?
Aya:	I am, but less than before. I'm only there 4( ) now. It's less money, but I'm happier.
Daniel:	I'm glad to hear it.

B. Choose the best answer.

1. (   ) Aya ____________ her new classes.
   A: doesn't like   B: rarely attends
   C: isn't sure about   D: enjoys

2. (   ) Which of these is probably true?
   A: Aya has more homework than last year.
   B: Daniel and Aya are in the same classes.
   C: Aya used to work more than two days a week.
   D: Daniel just met Aya a few days ago.

Discussion

Discuss these questions together.

1. How often do you see your close friends?
2. What do you and your friends do for fun?
3. Is it easy to make new friends at school?

5 Helping Others

Part 1: Volunteering

Read the following article. Track 10

Anyone can be a volunteer. It's a great way to help others. Plus, it doesn't matter how old you are.

There are many ways to volunteer. You can help at a library or school. Or you might spend time with older people. You could also clean your neighborhood's streets and parks.

There is usually a big need for volunteers. It only takes a small amount of time each week. In return, you receive many smiles and thanks.

Vocabulary Check

Write the correct word in each blank.

smile	neighborhood	library	received

1. What time does the ____________ open? I need to return a book.
2. Do you like my watch? I ____________ it as a graduation present.
3. Your mother has such a friendly ____________.
4. This ____________ is full of songbirds. There are some in that tree right there.

Reading Check

Choose the best answer.

1. (   ) Volunteers ___________.
   A: are always adults
   B: may be any age
   C: mostly help at libraries
   D: are not often needed

2. (   ) What payment do volunteers get?
   A: A lot of money
   B: The thanks of other people
   C: Food and other items
   D: Some money, but not much

3. (   ) What does "it doesn't matter" mean?
   A: it's not popular
   B: it's not right
   C: it's not possible
   D: it's not important

4. (   ) Which of these types of volunteering is not mentioned?
   A: Cleaning one's neighborhood
   B: Keeping older people company
   C: Reading books to young people
   D: Spending time at a school

Grammar Check

Put the words in the correct order.

1. (people / like to / animal shelters / Many / help at)

   ____.

2. (are / beach / Some / cleaning / the / students)

   ____.

3. (to /we / do / sign up / volunteer / Where)

   ____?

Part 2: How People Volunteer

Read the following information.

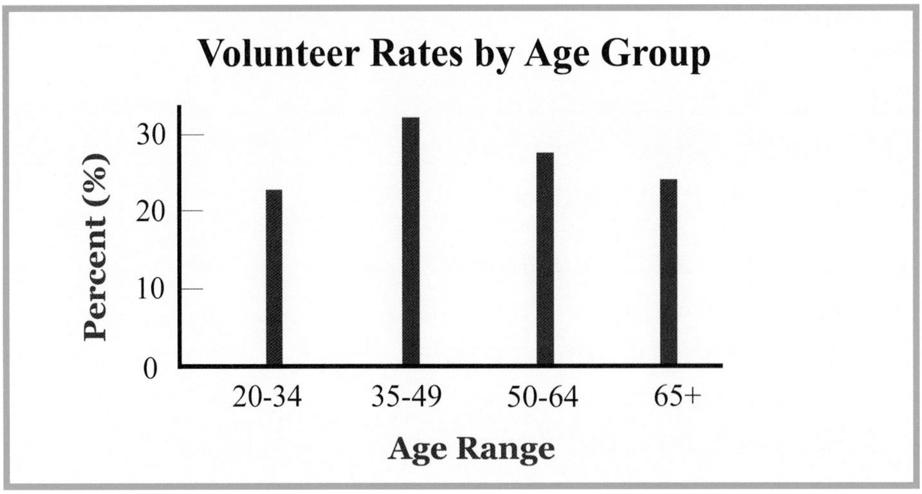

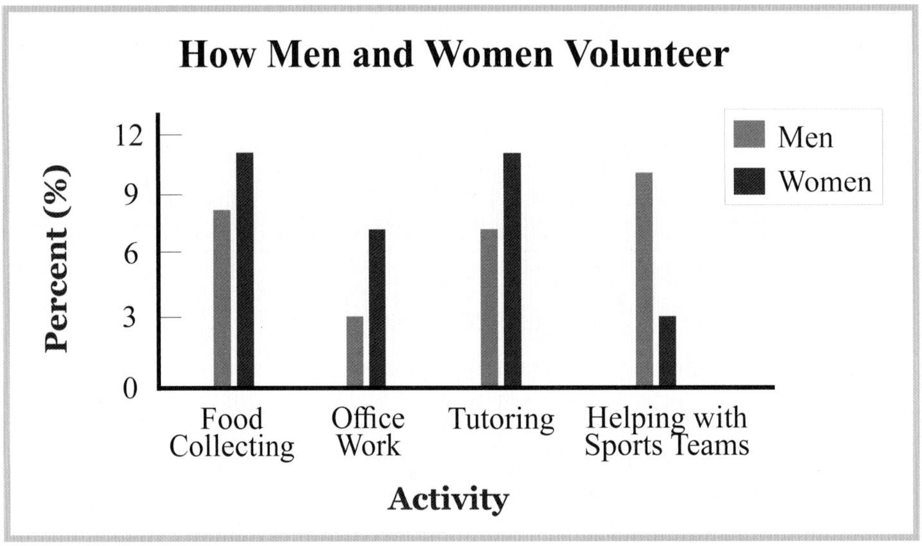

True or False

Circle true (T) or false (F).

1. (T/F) About 30% of people in the 20-34 age group volunteer.

2. (T/F) The 35-49 age group has the highest volunteer rate.

3. (T/F) For men, food collecting is the most popular way to volunteer.

4. (T/F) Women volunteer for office work more than men do.

Dictation

A. Listen and fill in the blanks. Track 11

Pierre: 1(   ) this Saturday? I just got some new video games.

Lydia: Sounds fun, but I'm afraid I can't. I volunteer at an animal shelter on Saturdays.

Pierre: I didn't know that. Is it for 2(   )?

Lydia: Mostly, but sometimes we get rabbits and birds. All the animals used to be pets. So there aren't any wild animals.

Pierre: Do they 3(   ) visitors?

Lydia: They sure do. If you want, you can even 4(   ). They always need volunteers.

B. Choose the best answer.

1. (   ) Lydia does not say the animal shelter helps ________.
   A: rabbits   B: dogs
   C: snakes   D: cats

2. (   ) What do we learn about the shelter?
   A: Some of the animals are wild.
   B: The staff all like video games.
   C: Pierre goes there every week.
   D: They are looking for volunteers.

Discussion

Discuss these questions together.

1. Have you ever volunteered? If so, what for? If not, would you like to?
2. In your area, is there a need for volunteers? What for?
3. Should everybody volunteer? Why or why not?

6 Traveling

Part 1: Niagara Falls

Read the following article. Track 12

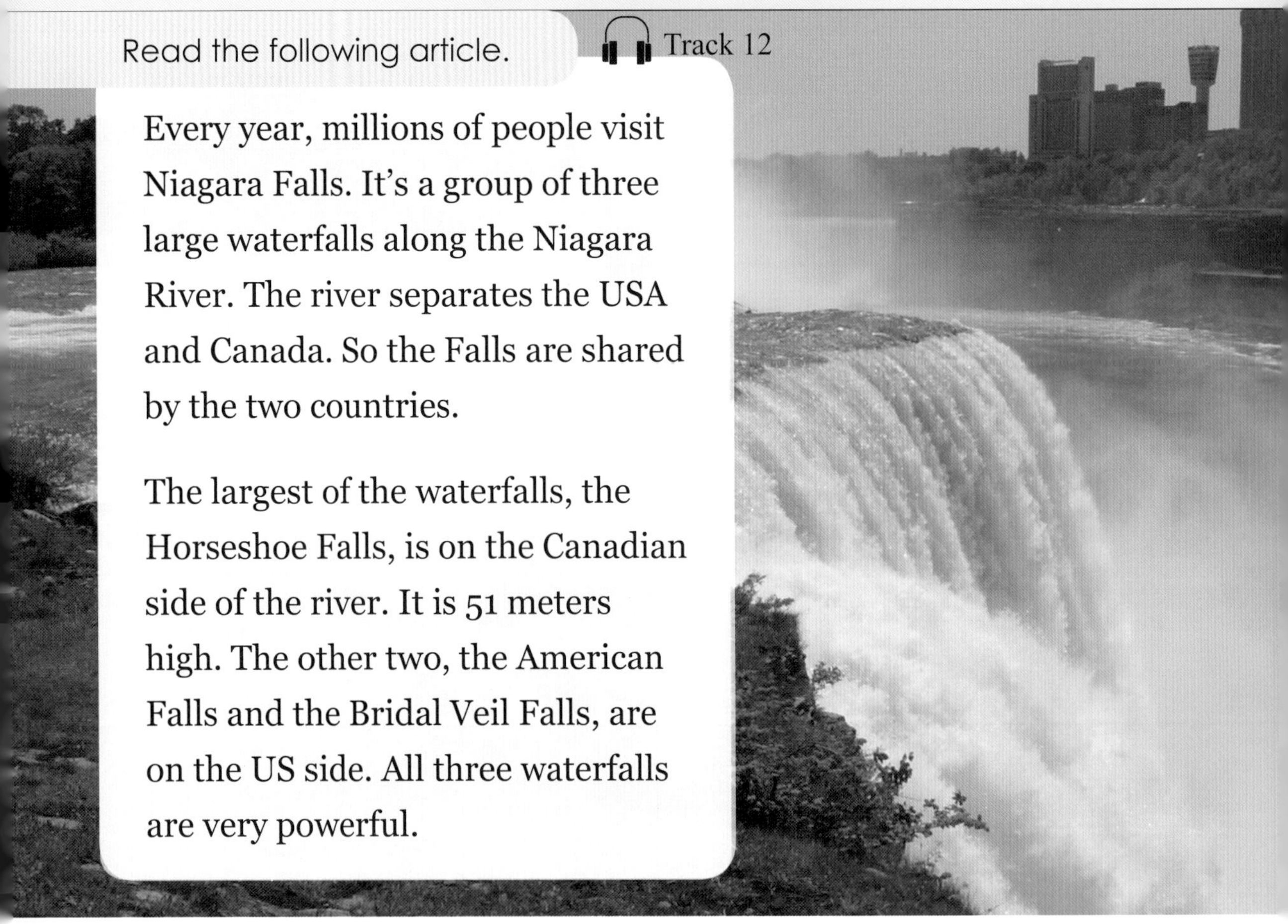

Every year, millions of people visit Niagara Falls. It's a group of three large waterfalls along the Niagara River. The river separates the USA and Canada. So the Falls are shared by the two countries.

The largest of the waterfalls, the Horseshoe Falls, is on the Canadian side of the river. It is 51 meters high. The other two, the American Falls and the Bridal Veil Falls, are on the US side. All three waterfalls are very powerful.

Vocabulary Check

Write the correct word in each blank.

along	side	share	powerful

1. This sandwich is too big. Do you want to ____________ it with me?

2. There are rose bushes all ____________ 5th Street. It's very pretty.

3. Please put the sofa on the other ____________ of the room.

4. Elephants are ____________ animals. They can even pull trees with their trunks.

Reading Check

Choose the best answer.

1. (   ) Where is the Niagara River?
   A: Next to millions of cities
   B: Near the world's largest waterfall
   C: In between the USA and Canada
   D: Close to Canada but far from the USA

2. (   ) What does the article suggest about the Bridal Veil Falls?
   A: It is more than 51 meters tall.
   B: It is not as tall as the Horseshoe Falls.
   C: It is on the Canadian side of the river.
   D: It is the same size as the American Falls.

3. (   ) In the first paragraph, what does "separates" mean?
   A: causes problems
   B: divides
   C: enters
   D: is near

4. (   ) Which of the following is true?
   A: Only one of Niagara's waterfalls is very powerful.
   B: The width of the waterfalls changes every month.
   C: The American Falls is smaller than the Horseshoe Falls.
   D: The Horseshoe Falls and the American Falls are on the same side of the river.

Grammar Check

Write the correct form of each verb.
Use the present tense.

Ex: We ___*visit*___ (visit) our grandmother once a year.

1. He __________ (swim) in the ocean every week.

2. People __________ (love) taking photos of waterfalls.

3. Some of the jackets __________ (be) made of wool.

4. She __________ (like) studying in Vancouver.

Part 2: Central Springfield

Look at the following map.

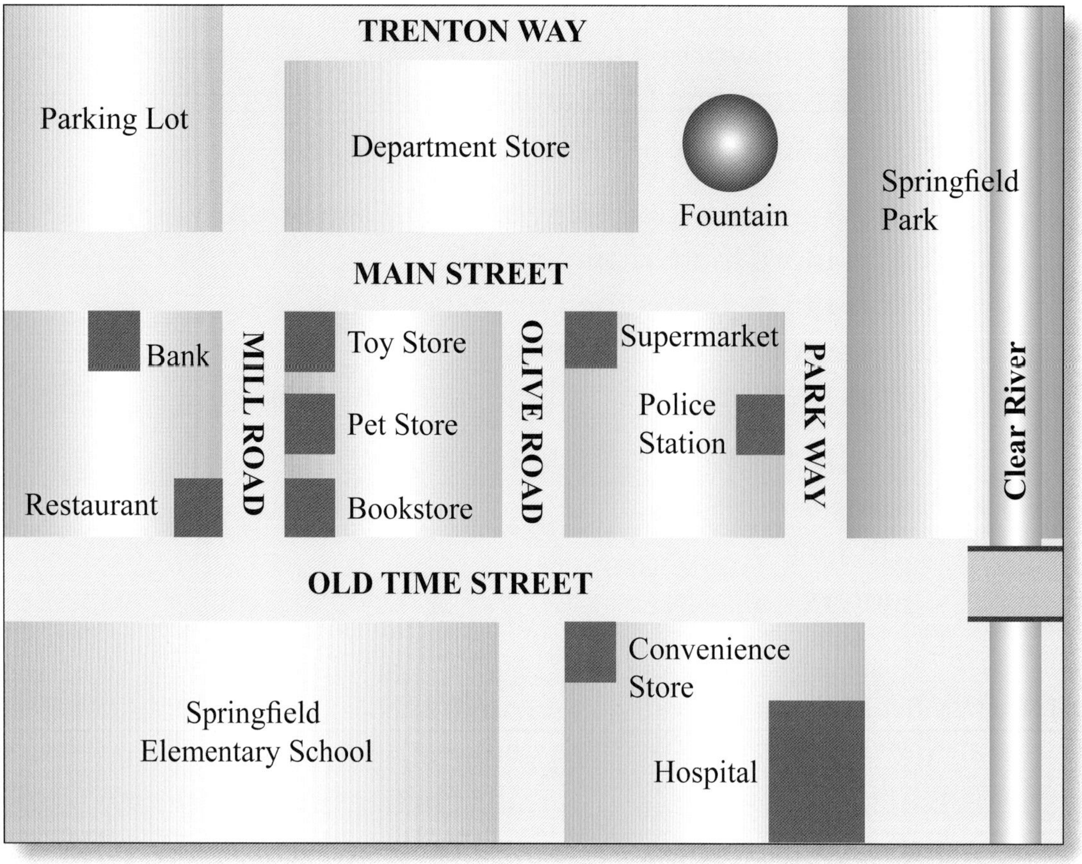

True or False

Circle true (T) or false (F).

1. (T/F) The pet store is in between the toy store and the bookstore.
2. (T/F) The convenience store is on the corner of Old Time Street and Olive Road.
3. (T/F) The police station is across the street from the restaurant.
4. (T/F) There are two rivers going through Springfield.

Dictation

A. Listen and fill in the blanks. Track 13

Steve: How was your trip to Egypt?

Dana: Incredible! The pyramids were amazing. I loved the $_{1}$(   ) and restaurants, too.

Steve: I saw the $_{2}$(   ) you posted online. Did you really ride a camel?

Dana: I did, and it ran $_{3}$(   )! I was afraid of falling off. Fortunately, someone was riding with me.

Steve: What an experience. I'd love to visit one day.

Dana: I'm sure you'll $_{4}$(   ).

B. Choose the best answer.

1. (   ) Dana did not ____________.
   A: go shopping B: travel to Egypt
   C: fall off a camel D: visit the pyramids

2. (   ) What do we learn about Steve?
   A: He shared his trip photos online.
   B: He is not interested in traveling.
   C: He had an experience like Dana's.
   D: He has never been to Egypt.

Discussion

Discuss these questions together.

1. What interesting places have you visited?
2. What do you like to do during trips? (Ex: eat new things, visit museums)
3. When you go somewhere new, how do you get information about the place? (Ex: from a guidebook, from a website)

7 Collections and Gifts

Part 1: Antiques

Read the following article. Track 14

Every new thing slowly becomes old. Things that are at least 20 years old are considered antiques. Anything can be an antique: cars, books, handmade clothes, and so on. Looking at and owning these items gives people a special feeling.

Some antiques are valuable. Collectors buy them and take good care of them. They put them in their homes and offices. Museums display very old antiques. That way, everybody can enjoy them. By studying antiques, we can even learn about our past.

Vocabulary Check

Write the correct word in each blank.

display	valuable	feeling	museum

1. The ring is ____________. It's made of gold.
2. On this shelf, I ____________ the things I collect.
3. This old house gives me a strange ____________.
4. Do you want to go to the art ____________ with me?

Reading Check

Choose the best answer.

1. (   ) To be an antique, an item must be ________.
   A: worth a lot of money   B: in a museum
   C: at least 20 years old   D: very popular

2. (   ) What would a collector probably do with an antique?
   A: Find a nice place to put it
   B: Give it to a young child
   C: Leave it in the rain
   D: Take it apart to recycle it

3. (   ) What good point about antiques is not mentioned?
   A: They remind us of our childhood.
   B: They are sometimes valuable.
   C: They can teach us about history.
   D: They might be handmade.

4. (   ) Why do museums display old antiques?
   A: To let everyone see them in person
   B: To compare them with new items
   C: To give people a chance to use them
   D: To stop collectors from buying them

Grammar Check

Write the correct word or words in each blank.

Ex: The store has ___*many*___ **more lamps upstairs.**
(much / many)

1. Fragile antiques need ____________ special care.
   (much/a lot of)

2. ____________ people like swimming in the rain.
   (Some/Much)

3. Wow, you have so ____________ cats!
   (many/lots)

4. I'm sorry, I dont have ____________ time to talk today.
   (many/much)

Look at the following receipt.

Gift Palace
2333 Blossom Road
San Jose, CA 95030

Item	Quantity	Price
Set of collectible glasses	1	$17.50
Picture frame	1	$7.50
Roll of tape	2	$2.00 each
Lion stuffed animal	1	$15.00
Roll of gift wrap	1	$3.00
Subtotal		$47.00
Tax (9.25%)		$4.35
Total		$51.35

True or False

Circle true (T) or false (F).

1. (T/F) The receipt is from a store on Gift Palace Road.
2. (T/F) The customer buys two rolls of tape.
3. (T/F) The set of glasses is the most expensive item.
4. (T/F) The customer brought $65 to the store. After these purchases, he or she has enough for another picture frame.

Dictation

A. Listen and fill in the blanks. Track 15

Mr. Lowell: How do you like the sunglasses? They're a 1( ) present from your uncle.

Darlene: They're awesome! They'll go great with my new hat.

Mr. Lowell: Remember to call him and thank him. So, 2( ) do you have planned for today?

Darlene: I'm 3( ) with some classmates. Then they're taking me ice skating.

Mr. Lowell: Now those are some good friends. You know we're having a big dinner tonight. Your mom is making a 4( ).

Darlene: I can't wait. I'll be back by 6:00.

B. Choose the best answer.

1. ( ) Darlene's ________ bought her a pair of sunglasses.
   A: classmate B: uncle
   C: mother D: father

2. ( ) What will Darlene do first?
   A: Return home
   B: Go ice skating
   C: Have some cake
   D: Eat lunch

Discussion

Discuss these questions together.

1. Do you own any antiques?
2. Do you collect anything? (Ex: coins, sports cards, toy figures)
3. What kinds of things do you often give as gifts? (Ex: clothes, chocolate)

Part 1: Modern Heroes

Read the following article. Track 16

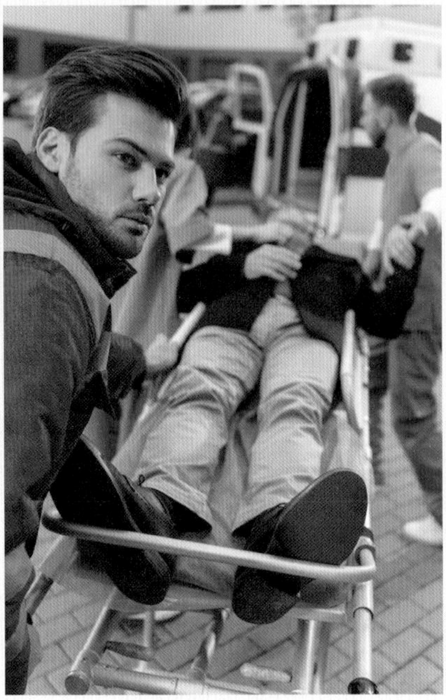

First responders, including fire fighters, police officers, and paramedics, are our modern heroes. They work day and night, on weekends and holidays, to keep us safe. And they are the first people to arrive at an emergency.

It takes a special man or woman to do such a hard job. Putting out a fire or catching a thief can be dangerous. Helping people who are hurt and rushing them to hospitals is difficult. But someone has to do it. So the next time you see one of these modern heroes, thank them. Tell them you appreciate their hard work.

Vocabulary Check

Write the correct word in each blank.

includes	dangerous	catch	appreciate

1. Don't climb the wall like that. It's ______________.

2. The dog is running away. Quick, ______________ it!

3. Thank you very much. I ______________ your help.

4. The set of dishes ______________ six plates and six bowls.

Reading Check

Choose the best answer.

1. (   ) First responders ____________.
   A: have very simple jobs
   B: don't often work on Saturday or Sunday
   C: help keep people safe
   D: arrive at emergencies after everyone else

2. (   ) How does the article describe fire fighters?
   A: Brave and hard-working   B: Slow and selfish
   C: Easy-going and safe   D: Unfriendly and boring

3. (   ) What is suggested about police officers' work?
   A: Being an officer is rarely dangerous.
   B: The job is hard, but it needs to be done.
   C: It's easier than being a fire fighter.
   D: Catching thieves is the main part of the job.

4. (   ) According to the article, what should we say to paramedics?
   A: "Thank you for everything you do."
   B: "What's the hardest thing about your job?"
   C: "Do you make a lot of money doing that?"
   D: "I'd love a free medical checkup!"

Grammar Check

Write the correct word or words in each blank.

Ex: Would you like ___*to have*___ **some of this pizza?**
(have / to have)

1. I love ______________ along the river.
   (walk/walking)

2. We should ______________ someone for help.
   (call/to call)

3. ______________ on holidays is no fun at all.
   (Work/Working)

4. Did the package ______________ on time?
   (arrive/to arrive)

Part 2: Seeing a Doctor

Read the following conversation.

True or False

Circle true (T) or false (F).

1. (T/F) The patient's problems started a week ago.
2. (T/F) The sick man probably has a cold.
3. (T/F) The doctor gives the man some medicine.
4. (T/F) The patient is told to avoid spicy food.

Dictation

A. Listen and fill in the blanks. Track 17

Maurice: My sister is working late again. That's 1(   ) this week.

Yolanda: Being a nurse must be tough.

Maurice: It is, but Carol loves it. She helps 2(   ).

Yolanda: Do you think her patients appreciate her?

Maurice: Most do. After they 3(   ), some people send her presents – stuff like cards and chocolates. They sometimes go back and visit her, too.

Yolanda: That's awesome. Hey, let's take Carol 4(   ) sometime. She deserves it.

B. Choose the best answer.

1. (   ) Maurice does not say patients ________ his sister.
   A: appreciate   B: buy dinner for
   C: give chocolates to   D: send cards to

2. (   ) What do we learn about Carol?
   A: She works at two hospitals.
   B: She is often visited by Yolanda.
   C: She sometimes has to work late.
   D: She sees her brother every week.

Discussion

Discuss these questions together.

1. Some jobs that focus on helping people are hard. Would you like to work as a first responder? Why or why not?
2. In your opinion, why do many people choose that type of career?
3. What's your idea of a perfect job?

9 European Cultures

Part 1: The Culture of Spain: Siestas

Read the following article. Track 18

In the south of Spain, siestas are an important part of the local culture. A siesta is a period of rest. During the siesta, from around 1:30 to 4:30 PM, many businesses close their doors. People go home to rest or eat. Afterwards, they go back to work.

The south of Spain gets very hot. Highs of 30-35 degrees are common in the summer. Siestas are a way to get away from the heat. Not every business follows this old custom, but many do.

Vocabulary Check

Write the correct word in each blank.

culture	during	custom	local

1. What do you do ____________ your afternoon break?
2. I checked the ____________ weather report. It should be sunny here all day.
3. The Chinese ____________ of eating with chopsticks is very old.
4. Understanding a country's ____________ helps us understand its people.

Reading Check

Choose the best answer.

1. (   ) During siestas, people ___________.
   A: work hard
   B: open their businesses
   C: take a rest at home
   D: go to church

2. (   ) How long do siestas last?
   A: About three hours
   B: Most of the year
   C: Just a few minutes
   D: Until 1:30 PM

3. (   ) Why do people take siestas?
   A: They work too hard in the morning.
   B: They have so much housework to finish.
   C: They are following the custom of every business.
   D: They want to take a break from the heat.

4. (   ) Which of the following is not true?
   A: Some offices stay open after 1:30.
   B: Siestas are common in every part of Spain.
   C: Siestas take place in the afternoon.
   D: The custom of taking siestas is old.

Grammar Check

Put the words in the correct order.

1. (are / about / art / learning / We / Dutch)

   ____.

2. (on / businesses / Many / closed / Sunday / are)

   ____.

3. (lasts / lunch break / hour / one / Our)

   ____.

Part 2: Friends in Paris

Read the following e-mail.

To: ftours@excite.com

From: caroline_strass@freemail.com

Subject: See you soon!

Hi Florence,

Everything is on schedule for my trip to France. I'm really excited, but also a little tired from all the planning. OK, here's an update. I've got my plane ticket. Tomorrow, I'll make my hotel reservation.

Let me give you my flight details so we can meet at the airport. I'll arrive in Paris at 5:40 PM on March 16, on Lufthansa flight LH 1040.

It's going to be so much fun spending time together! When is the last time we met up? Let me think.…Wow, it was seven years ago in Auckland. This time, you can show me around Paris. And I can finally meet your bird Paulie.

Well, I'll see you soon!

Caroline

True or False

Circle true (T) or false (F).

1. (T/ F) Caroline saw Florence in France seven years ago.
2. (T/ F) Caroline still needs to book her hotel room.
3. (T/ F) Paulie and Caroline are old friends.
4. (T/ F) Florence will meet Caroline at the airport.

Dictation

A. Listen and fill in the blanks. Track 19

Anne: How was your 1(   ) in Italy?

Matt: Really good. I was in a 2(   ) in the countryside. It's a different world over there.

Anne: I bet the food was incredible.

Matt: It was. And the people were so open. They 3(   ) everything, even with new friends. It took a while to get used to.

Anne: What an amazing experience. Do you want to go back?

Matt: Maybe 4(   ), after I graduate.

B. Choose the best answer.

1. (   ) What was challenging for Matt in Italy?
   A: Getting used to people's openness
   B: Learning to cook Italian food
   C: Traveling around the countryside
   D: Having fun without speaking Italian

2. (   ) How does Matt feel about returning to Italy?
   A: He plans to travel there this year.
   B: He isn't interested in going back.
   C: He might like to return one day.
   D: He wants to wait until Anne graduates.

Discussion

Discuss these questions together.

1. Are you interested in any European cultures? If so, which ones?

2. What's a good way to learn about another culture?

3. What do people from other countries like about your culture?

10 Gifted Children

Part 1: Child Prodigies

Read the following article. Track 20

Child prodigies are very special children. Early on – as young as two or three years old – they become skilled at certain things. They learn quickly, often without trying hard.

There are child prodigies in many fields, like music, math, sports, and art. Two famous examples are Mozart in music and Tiger Woods in golf.

Life isn't always easy for these talented children. People expect great things from them. They are often under pressure to practice and show their skills. It's hard to balance being a genius and being a kid.

Vocabulary Check

Write the correct word in each blank.

famous	life	pressure	young

1. The soccer star is a __________ person. Almost everybody knows his face.
2. The little boy can't go into the bar. He's too __________.
3. My grandfather enjoys his slow and peaceful __________.
4. Students often feel __________ before a big test.

Reading Check

Choose the best answer.

1. (　　) Child prodigies ＿＿＿＿＿＿ .
   A: take many years to become good at something
   B: may have great talent at three years of age
   C: have the same skill level as other children
   D: are often good at sports or math, but not music

2. (　　) What trouble do child prodigies have?
   A: They don't usually have any friends.
   B: Other people expect a lot from them.
   C: Child prodigies don't like being smart.
   D: The world doesn't understand them.

3. (　　) Why does the article mention Tiger Woods?
   A: To teach us about golf
   B: To show how he is different from Mozart
   C: To tell us about a math genius
   D: To give an example of a child prodigy

4. (　　) In the third paragraph, who or what are "they"?
   A: adults
   B: special skills
   C: great things
   D: child prodigies

Grammar Check

Complete each sentence with *to*, *for*, or *at*.

Ex: Is Ryosei still ＿＿*at*＿＿ work?

1. You are so good ＿＿＿＿＿＿ designing T-shirts!

2. All parents want their children ＿＿＿＿＿＿ have a good life.

3. These shoes are great ＿＿＿＿＿＿ rock climbing.

4. One day, I hope ＿＿＿＿＿＿ become a musician.

Part 2: What makes a prodigy?

Read the following table of contents.

Contents

All about Child Prodigies

Contents

True or False

Circle true (T) or false (F).

1. (T/F) On page 20, you might read about a tennis prodigy.

2. (T/F) In Part 2, you can read about prodigies' parents.

3. (T/F) Marie Curie was a prodigy in several fields.

4. (T/F) The chapter on Blaise Pascal is 16 pages long.

Dictation

A. Listen and fill in the blanks. Track 21

Maya: Stephanie plays the piano so beautifully. 1( ) she's only seven?

Trevor: That's what the program says. She received her first piano on her third birthday.

Maya: She must practice 2( ). I hope Stephanie has time to have fun. Does the program say anything about that?

Trevor: Yes, it says she loves 3( ) with her two brothers.

Maya: That's good. Being that talented is great. But children 4( ) to be, well...children.

Trevor: I think so, too.

B. Choose the best answer.

1. ( ) Stephanie started playing the piano at the age of ________.
   A: two B: three C: five D: seven

2. ( ) What does Maya say about Stephanie?
   A: She is probably a good bike rider.
   B: She doesn't have any fun.
   C: She practices playing the piano a lot.
   D: She has intelligent brothers.

Discussion

Discuss these questions together.

1. As a child, what did you do for fun?

2. What's good about being a child prodigy?

3. Is there anything bad about being a prodigy?

11 Restaurants

Part 1: Helping at the Family Business

Read the following story. Track 22

Peter's family owns a restaurant. His mother and father work there almost every day. Several days a week (after school and on the weekend), Peter goes to the restaurant. He does his homework in the back room.

Sometimes, the restaurant is full of people. Peter's mother and father need his help. He cleans tables and brings water to customers. Peter also helps in the kitchen. He really likes that. He gets to taste many delicious kinds of food.

Vocabulary Check

Write the correct word in each blank.

taste	delicious	customers	own

1. The pizza is so ____________. I could eat here every day.

2. I want to ____________ a big truck someday.

3. Here, ____________ this vegetable soup.

4. The popular bakery is always full of ____________.

Reading Check

Choose the best answer.

1. ( ) Peter is a ___________ son.
   A: lazy B: bored
   C: helpful D: full

2. ( ) How often does Peter go to the restaurant?
   A: A few times a week
   B: Every day
   C: On Saturday and Sunday only
   D: Just on holidays

3. ( ) Peter does not ___________.
   A: help in the kitchen
   B: clean tables
   C: bring people water
   D: take customers' orders

4. ( ) Which of the following is true?
   A: Peter rarely does his homework.
   B: Peter's parents bring him to the restaurant.
   C: The restaurant is never busy.
   D: Working in the kitchen is fun for Peter.

Grammar Check

Write the correct word in each blank.

Ex: I eat at this noodle shop almost *every* **day.**
(every / most)

1. We go shopping there ___________ a week.
   (one/once)

2. ___________ mornings, the coffee shop is full of customers.
   (Most/Much)

3. My parents are so busy. They work ___________ the time.
   (all/every)

4. The food is fresh and well made. It's ___________ delicious.
   (rarely/always)

Part 2: A Taste of Italy

Read the following conversation.

Server: Are you ready to order?

Customer: Yes, I'd like a cheese pizza and a Coke, please.

Server: Would you like a soup or salad to go with that?

Customer: A salad sounds good.

Server: Then you should get the special. For $12, you can get a pizza, drink, and soup or salad.

Customer: That’s a good deal. Please give me the special, with a salad.

Server: Sure thing.

Customer: Thanks very much.

Server: You’re welcome.

A Taste of Italy

Soup

Black Bean	$3.50
Vegetable	$4.00

Salad

Small Salad	$4.25
Large Salad	$7.50

Pizza

Cheese	$8.50
Sausage	$10.00
Combo	$11.50

Drinks

Coke	$2.75
Iced Tea	$2.75
Coffee	$2.50

True or False

Circle true (T) or false (F).

1. (T/F) It costs less than $10 to buy a Coke and a combo pizza.
2. (T/F) The restaurant has three kinds of pizza.
3. (T/F) The customer does not want anything to drink.
4. (T/F) The server helps the customer save money.

Dictation

A. Listen and fill in the blanks. Track 23

Sean: It's just about dinner time. There are some amazing restaurants 1(   ). What are you in the mood for?

Sandy: 2(   ). That pasta lunch was delicious, and so was dessert. But it filled me up.

Sean: Me, too. How about Greek food? There's a new place about 3(   ). It's getting great reviews.

Sandy: That could be nice. I love Greek salad. That and some pita bread would be perfect. Do they have outdoor seating?

Sean: 4(   ) – they have rooftop seating.

Sandy: Wonderful! Let's try it.

B. Choose the best answer.

1. (   ) Sandy would like to eat ________.
   A: Italian food   B: at home
   C: a salad   D: inside

2. (   ) Why do they want a light dinner?
   A: They already had a big lunch and dessert.
   B: They need to be home soon.
   C: They never eat big dinners.
   D: They ate Greek food earlier in the day.

Discussion

Discuss these questions together.

1. What's your favorite meal of the day – breakfast, lunch, or dinner?
2. How often do you eat out?
3. What's your favorite restaurant?

12 Transportation

Part 1: River Taxis

Read the following article. Track 24

In Thailand, a country full of rivers, river taxis are a good way to get around. These boats act much like buses on city streets. People wait at a boat stop on the riverside. The boats stop to let people on and off.

In some of Thailand's cities, street traffic can get heavy. Using a river taxi is a big time saver. For example, many boats go up and down the Chao Phraya River in Bangkok. A number of Bangkok's interesting sites are near the river. Taking a boat is a great way for visitors to see parts of the city.

Vocabulary Check

Write the correct word in each blank.

visitors	traffic	boat	river

1. Downtown ____________ gets bad at 5:00 PM.

2. Many colorful fish are swimming in the ____________.

3. ____________ to our town enjoy the toy museum.

4. There is room for 25 people on the ____________.

Reading Check

Choose the best answer.

1. (   ) Why are river taxis like buses?
   A: Both are free for local riders.
   B: Both have wheels.
   C: Both let you on and off at special stops.
   D: Both go along city streets.

2. (   ) Visitors to Bangkok ____________.
   A: don't understand how to use river taxis
   B: like to swim in the Chao Phraya River
   C: find river taxis convenient for sightseeing
   D: try hard to see the whole city in one day

3. (   ) What does "up and down" mean?
   A: in both directions
   B: at all times
   C: around and around
   D: in and out

4. (   ) Which of the following is not true?
   A: River taxis are a helpful way for visitors to see sites.
   B: Bangkok's traffic isn't always smooth.
   C: There are rivers in many parts of Thailand.
   D: You can get on a river taxi anywhere along a river.

Grammar Check

Complete each sentence with *in*, *on*, or *at*.

Ex: I fell asleep ____*on*____ the plane.

1. The streets ____________ Beijing are wide.

2. Let's hurry and get ____________ the train.

3. The stadium is up ahead. We'll get off ____________ the next stop.

4. Is Kyle's house ____________ this street?

Part 2: Traffic Safety

Read the following information.

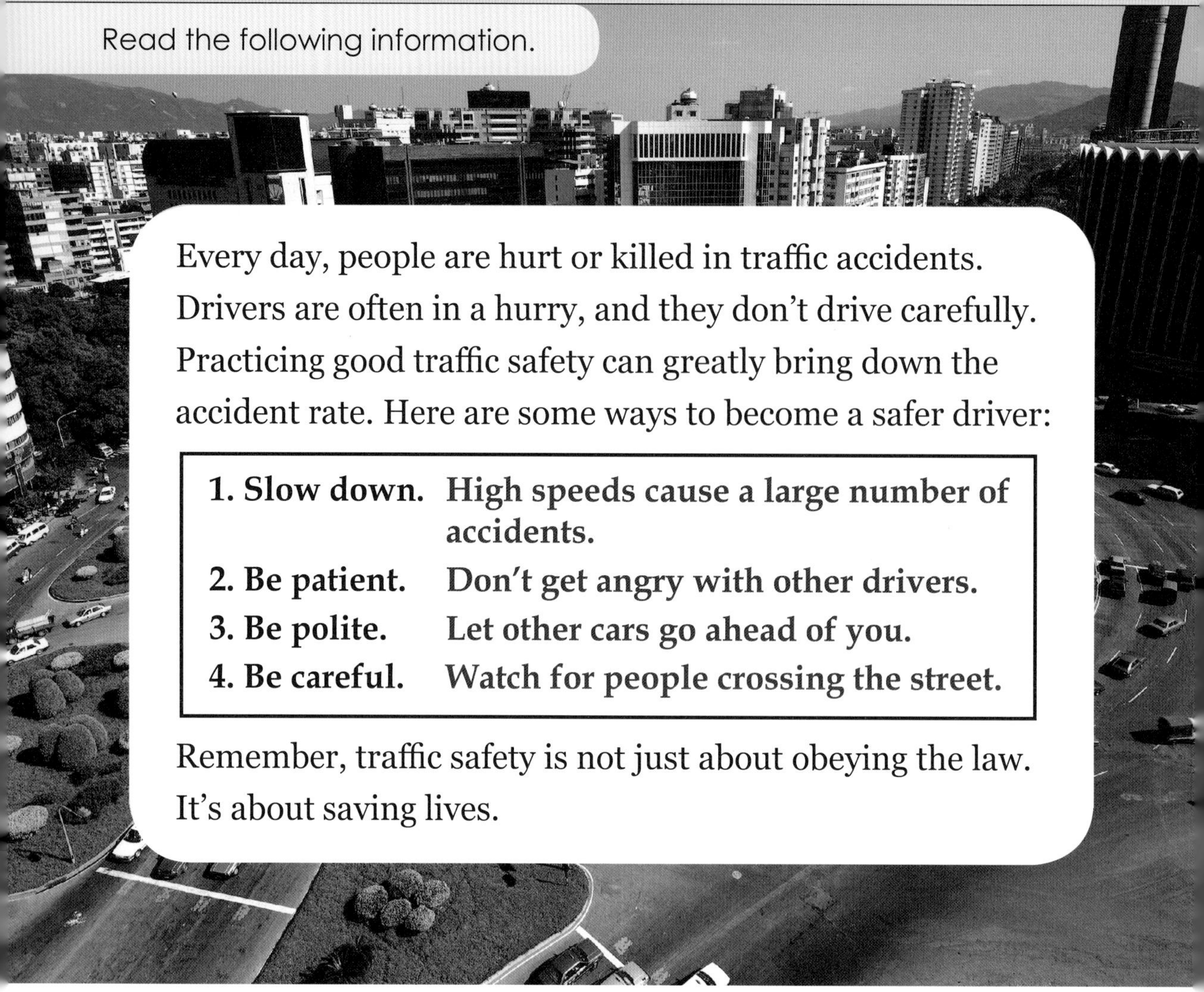

Every day, people are hurt or killed in traffic accidents. Drivers are often in a hurry, and they don't drive carefully. Practicing good traffic safety can greatly bring down the accident rate. Here are some ways to become a safer driver:

1. Slow down.	**High speeds cause a large number of accidents.**
2. Be patient.	**Don't get angry with other drivers.**
3. Be polite.	**Let other cars go ahead of you.**
4. Be careful.	**Watch for people crossing the street.**

Remember, traffic safety is not just about obeying the law. It's about saving lives.

True or False

Circle true (T) or false (F).

1. (T/F) The article says being patient causes accidents.

2. (T/F) In the first paragraph, "bring down" means "lower."

3. (T/F) The only reason to drive safely is to obey the law.

4. (T/F) To be careful, watch for people crossing the street.

Dictation

A. Listen and fill in the blanks. Track 25

Pamela: Why are you $_1$(   ) so fast?

George: The game starts in 15 minutes. I want to get home before then.

Pamela: I know you really want to $_2$(   ). But we're going a little too fast. At this speed, you'll only save two or three minutes.

George: Oh, sorry. You're probably $_3$(   ). I can miss the first five minutes of the game.

Pamela: Thanks for slowing down. Hey, $_4$(   ), should I make some popcorn?

George: Yes, please – with butter!

B. Choose the best answer.

1. (   ) Let's say George does not slow down. He may get home __________ minutes faster than usual.
   A: 3   B: 5   C: 15   D: 20

2. (   ) What will Pamela do at their house?
   A: Play a game   B: Drive somewhere slowly
   C: Prepare something to eat   D: Watch a movie

Discussion

Discuss these questions together.

1. Besides river taxis, what are some other interesting ways to get around?
2. Why are car drivers often in a hurry?
3. Soon, many cars may drive themselves. Will that make roads safer?

13 Homes

Part 1: Castles

Read the following article. Track 26

At one time in many places, kings, queens, and other leaders lived in castles. At first, castles were made of wood, but they easily burned down. Stone later became a more popular building material.

Castles were often built on hills to make them easier to defend. Large walls around the main buildings gave more protection. Most castles were small, but some, like Windsor Castle in England, were very large.

Usually, castles were not comfortable places to live, but that didn't matter. Their main jobs were to stop enemy attacks and protect the people inside.

Vocabulary Check

Write the correct word in each blank.

stone	comfortable	protect	enemy

1. I love your new sofa. It's so ____________.

2. I put a big ____________ on the stack of papers. They won't blow away.

3. Metal workers wear gloves to ____________ their hands.

4. The cat is a famous ____________ of the mouse.

Reading Check

Choose the best answer.

1. (　) Why did stone become a more popular building material?
   A: It was cheaper than wood.
   B: It didn't burn as easily as wood.
   C: It looked better than wood.
   D: It was easier to find than wood.

2. (　) Windsor Castle is an example of ________.
   A: a castle made of wood
   B: a castle on a hill
   C: a comfortable place to live
   D: a big castle

3. (　) What does "defend" mean?
   A: see　　B: attack
   C: build　　D: protect

4. (　) Castles on flat ground probably ________.
   A: are harder to defend than castles on a hill
   B: easily burn down
   C: all have large wooden walls around them
   D: are easy to build

Grammar Check

Write the correct word in each blank.

Ex: The seawall is a good *defense* **against storms.**
(defend / defense)

1. Which color are you going to ________?
   (choose/choice)

2. He lives in a really tall ________. It's 18 stories high.
   (build/building)

3. For extra ________, some castles were surrounded by water.
   (protect/protection)

4. My sister has an interesting ________.
   (live/life)

Part 2: Apartments for Rent

Read the following apartment ads.

A

Lovely little apartment in new building. One bedroom, one bathroom, living room. Furnished. 75,000 yen per month.

B

Large downtown apartment. One-minute walk to train station. Three bedrooms (two large, one small), two bathrooms, BIG kitchen. Partly furnished. 130,000 yen per month.

C

Studio for rent. Great for student or busy working person. 55,000 yen per month.

D

Two-story apartment in private community. Swimming pool, exercise room, 24-hour guard. Large play area for kids. 170,000 yen per month.

True or False

Circle true (T) or false (F).

1. (T/F) Apartment A costs less to rent than apartment D.
2. (T/F) For a university student, apartment C would be a nice choice.
3. (T/F) Apartment B is far from the noisy city.
4. (T/F) Kate and her family want a large, safe apartment. They also like to exercise. Apartment D might be a good choice for them.

Dictation

A. Listen and fill in the blanks. Track 27

Ellie: My apartment is 1(   ). I don't even have room for a desk.

Hideo: Have you thought about moving to a bigger place?

Ellie: I really want to. I checked online, but everything is so expensive. Plus, there are agent's fees and so many 2(   ).

Hideo: Hmm...My friend Richard just moved. He used an agent 3(   ). The apartment is nice. Also, there weren't a lot of costs.

Ellie: Can you get the agent's 4(   ) for me?

Hideo: Not a problem. I'll ask Richard tonight.

B. Choose the best answer.

1. (   ) Ellie wants to ____________.
   A: buy a computer
   B: find a roommate
   C: change apartments
   D: become an agent

2. (   ) What will Hideo do later?
   A: Ask a friend for information
   B: Have dinner with Richard
   C: Go to a store with Ellie
   D: Call a housing agent

Discussion

Discuss these questions together.

1. Have you ever visited a castle or other old building? If so, where was it?
2. What is your idea of a dream home? (Ex: a big apartment in the city, a house in the countryside)
3. Do you plan to buy a home someday? Or will you be happy renting a place?

14 Space

Part 1: Space Tourism

Read the following article. Track 28

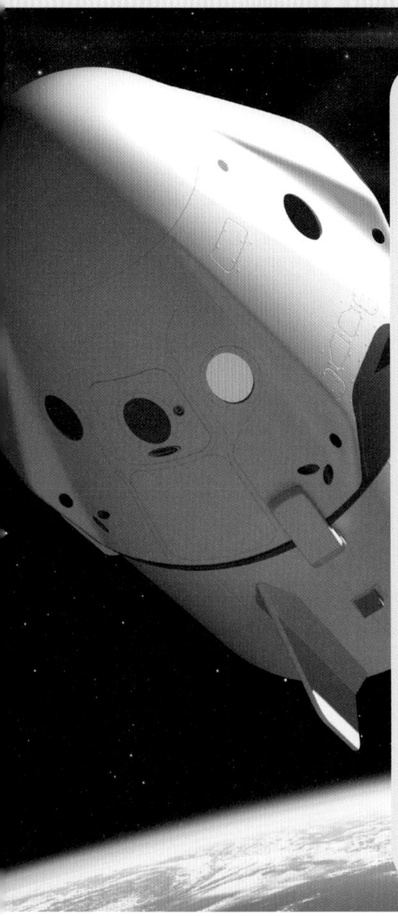

The first person flew into space in 1961. Shortly afterwards, in 1969, the first man walked on the moon. Incredible flights like these were enjoyed by just a few astronauts. The rest of us had to watch in wonder.

That is changing with the growth of space tourism. The first space tourists were rich. They paid a lot for flights on government-built ships. Now, several private companies are building spaceships. The first, SpaceShipOne, briefly flew into space in June, 2004.

Over the next 20 years, space flight will become cheaper and more common. Thousands of people are excitedly waiting for the chance.

Vocabulary Check

Write the correct word in each blank.

incredible	private	tourists	briefly

1. I only had a few minutes, so I spoke with him ____________.
2. The woman's story was ____________ . Nobody believed it.
3. ____________ in Taiwan love eating the delicious food.
4. I can't give you that information. It's ____________.

Reading Check

Choose the best answer.

1. (   ) What does the article suggest about space tourism?
   A: It will always be for the super-rich only.
   B: Few people are interested in space travel.
   C: It won't be possible for another 50 years.
   D: Many people would like to fly into space.

2. (   ) What is SpaceShipOne?
   A: A privately-built spaceship
   B: The ship that brought the first person into space
   C: The first government-built ship to reach the moon
   D: A spaceship built for one person

3. (   ) Who are "the rest of us"?
   A: people in government space programs
   B: common people
   C: very rich people
   D: people working on the first spaceships

4. (   ) What happened first?
   A: A man walked on the moon.
   B: SpaceShipOne made its historic flight.
   C: A ship carried someone into space.
   D: A rich tourist flew into space.

Grammar Check

Put the words in the correct order.

1. (high speeds / travel / Spaceships / very / at)

____.

2. (interested in / into space / you / a trip / Are / taking)

____?

3. (what / the moon / to walk on / wonder / I / it's like)

____.

Part 2: Poll about Space Travel

Look at the following poll.

This poll will help us understand people's feelings about space travel. Please check one answer for each question.

1. How interested are you in news about space?
   - ☐ Not very interested
   - ☐ Somewhat interested
   - ☐ Very interested
2. What type of trip into space would interest you the most?
   - ☐ A five-minute trip
   - ☐ A two or three-day trip
   - ☐ A trip lasting two weeks
3. What may be the most exciting thing about space travel?
   - ☐ Seeing the Earth from space
   - ☐ Floating in zero gravity
   - ☐ Exploring new things
4. What would be your greatest worry about space travel?
   - ☐ The safety of the trip
   - ☐ The high cost
   - ☐ Health problems after the trip

Current Results

1.	Not very interested	18%
	Somewhat interested	55%
	Very interested	27%
2.	A five-minute trip	48%
	A two or three-day trip	37%
	A trip lasting two weeks	15%
3.	Seeing the Earth from space	39%
	Floating in zero gravity	39%
	Exploring new things	22%
4.	The safety of the trip	45%
	The high cost	43%
	Health problems after the trip	12%

True or False

Circle true (T) or false (F).

1. (T/F) There is one question about poll takers' jobs.

2. (T/F) Less than half the people are interested in space news.

3. (T/F) A two-week trip would interest 15% of the people.

4. (T/F) Safety was the biggest worry of poll takers.

Dictation

A. Listen and fill in the blanks. Track 29

Patricia: Did you hear? A startup company 1(   ) a space hotel.

Nicholas: Is there a market for that sort of thing?

Patricia: It sounds like it. They already have reservations for 2(   ).

Nicholas: Is that so? I've always wanted to visit France. But I'm not sure about floating above 3(   ).

Patricia: I think it would be exciting. Hopefully the cost will go down. Anyway, building the hotel will take eight years.

Nicholas: I guess you have 4(   ) for the trip!

B. Choose the best answer.

1. (   ) Patricia suggests space hotel visits will be ________.
   A: expensive   B: dangerous
   C: unpopular   D: strange

2. (   ) What do we learn about Nicholas?
   A: He has visited 50 countries.
   B: He wants to take a trip to France.
   C: He used to live in Europe.
   D: He would love to float in space.

Discussion

Discuss these questions together.

1. Are you interested in a trip into space? Why or why not?
2. In the future, will many people live in space? Where might they live?
3. Should countries work together more on space programs? Or should each country focus on its own program?

15 Personality

Part 1: Habits

Read the following article. Track 30

Habits are an important part of our daily lives. They affect the time we go to sleep, the things we eat, and even the way we behave. Habits can be helpful. They save us time and energy. Thanks to habits, we don't have to think hard about every decision.

It's easy to form habits, but it can be hard to break them. Many people have bad habits, like sleeping too much and eating junk food. To break a bad habit, we need to be aware of it first. Then, we can try to change it.

Vocabulary Check

Write the correct word in each blank.

affects	behaves	decision	energy

1. We need to make a(n) ____________ about this case.
2. The little boy ____________ like a monkey. He's up in a tree again.
3. I've been up since 5:00 AM. I don't have any ____________ left.
4. Sometimes, the weather ____________ my mood.

Reading Check

Choose the best answer.

1. (   ) According to the article, __________ habits.
   A: only a few people have
   B: it's impossible to change
   C: there are good and bad
   D: we need to break all of our

2. (   ) How can habits be helpful?
   A: They always help us make good decisions.
   B: They save us time.
   C: They make us behave like better people.
   D: They let us sleep longer.

3. (   ) Why does the article mention eating junk food?
   A: To give an example of a healthy thing to eat
   B: To give an example of a good habit
   C: To give an example of a way to change our lives
   D: To give an example of a bad habit

4. (   ) What is another way to say "be aware of"?
   A: break   B: recognize
   C: form   D: forget

Grammar Check

Write the correct word in each blank.

Ex: I can get ready very ***quickly*** **. I just need five minutes.**
(quick / quickly)

1. Many people form habits __________.
   (easy/easily)

2. The driving test was a little __________. But I think I passed.
   (hard/hardly)

3. Not exercising enough is one of my __________ points.
   (weak/weakly)

4. I packed the glass dishes __________. They won't break.
   (careful/carefully)

Part 2: Feelings and Opinions

Read the following information.

Using credit cards is a common habit. What do you think about them?

Carlos I think they're great. I don't like carrying around too much cash. So I find credit cards convenient.

Monique In my opinion, they're dangerous. People aren't careful with their money. Lots of people spend more than they should.

Devon The way I see it, they can be good or bad. We need to be responsible with credit cards. Otherwise, they can be a problem.

Haruko I love my credit cards! I use them all the time. They're great for ordering movie tickets and buying things online. I can't imagine living without them.

True or False

Circle true (T) or false (F).

1. (T/F) Haruko and Monique have the same opinion.
2. (T/F) Carlos thinks people are not careful with credit cards.
3. (T/F) Devon has a balanced opinion. He thinks credit cards can be a good thing or a problem.
4. (T/F) Haruko probably carries a credit card in her purse.

Dictation

A. Listen and fill in the blanks. Track 31

Naomi: It's Saturday. That means it's time for some 1( )!

Pedro: Didn't you buy a new jacket last weekend?

Naomi: I sure did. I like to get something new every week. It keeps things 2( ) and interesting. Don't you have any habits like that?

Pedro: Let me think.... 3( ). I go out for ice cream with friends every Friday.

Naomi: See, there you go. Life is 4( ). We should treat ourselves better.

Pedro: Well said.

B. Choose the best answer.

1. ( ) Pedro meets his friends for ice cream ________.
   A: once a week B: every weekend
   C: most Saturdays D: almost daily

2. ( ) Why does Naomi buy new clothes so often?
   A: Shopping is her only hobby.
   B: It gives her a chance to see friends.
   C: She wants to have an interesting life.
   D: Fashions change all the time.

Discussion

Discuss these questions together.

1. What are some of your daily habits? (Ex: waking up at a certain time)
2. Do you have any bad habits? (Ex: staying up late)
3. Do you have any regular weekly activities? (Ex: eating at a certain restaurant, going out with the same friends)

16 Design and Fashion

Part 1: Persian Rugs

Read the following article. Track 32

Persian rugs are beautiful, traditional floor coverings. In the Middle East, South Asia, and East Asia, rug making is an art form going back hundreds of years. Different countries are famous for using special materials, colors, and designs.

The best rugs are handmade, using a machine called a loom. Rugs are usually made of wool. Some are made of silk, but they can be very expensive.

High-quality rugs are attractive and useful. They also last a long time. Well-cared-for rugs may last a hundred years or longer.

Vocabulary Check

Write the correct word in each blank.

quality	attractive	machine	material

1. What ______________ is the shirt made of? Is it cotton?
2. The dress is very ______________. I think you should buy it.
3. The table wasn't the best ______________. It broke after a month.
4. My computer is a useful ______________.

Reading Check

Choose the best answer.

1. (   ) Why are high-quality rugs good to own?
   A: They are more beautiful than cheap rugs.
   B: They always last hundreds of years.
   C: They are usually made of silk.
   D: They can be used for many years.

2. (   ) In different parts of the world, __________.
   A: rugs are almost exactly the same
   B: only the materials and colors of rugs are different
   C: rugs are made in a variety of designs
   D: rugs are always a home's most attractive item

3. (   ) What does "going back hundreds of years" mean?
   A: ending 200 or 300 years ago
   B: worth a lot for a long time
   C: made a very long time ago
   D: starting hundreds of years ago

4. (   ) What do people do with a loom?
   A: They make rugs.
   B: They make floors.
   C: They make wool.
   D: They make machines.

Grammar Check

Write the correct form of each word.

Ex: Rugs are ___*seen*___ (see) in many living rooms.

1. The bag was __________ (make) in Brazil.

2. Where can I have the rug __________ (clean)?

3. The tea set was __________ (give) to my sister on her birthday.

4. The wallpaper will be __________ (choose) by my wife.

Part 2: Clothes Shopping

Read the following conversation.

True or False

Circle true (T) or false (F).

1. (T/F) The customer is shopping for a present.
2. (T/F) The salesperson says silk ties are popular.
3. (T/F) The store only sells expensive ties.
4. (T/F) The customer buys something from Italy.

Dictation

A. Listen and fill in the blanks. Track 33

Ronda: I love my new apartment, but it's nearly 1( ). I need some more furniture.

Darren: There's a big furniture store in Westwood Mall.

Ronda: I 2( ) there. It's not quite my style. I'm looking for tables and chairs made of solid wood.

Darren: How about something handmade?

Ronda: That would be 3( )!

Darren: My cousin Timothy knows some artists and craftspeople. They build 4( ). It might be a good option for you.

B. Choose the best answer.

1. ( ) Ronda is looking for ________.
   - A: new furniture B: some roommates
   - C: an apartment D: a ride to the mall

2. ( ) Who might build something?
   - A: Ronda B: Darren's cousin
   - C: Darren D: Timothy's friends

Discussion

Discuss these questions together.

1. How do you decorate your home? Do you have posters on the wall, rugs on the floor, etc.?
2. Some people like simple, basic furniture. Other people like beautiful furniture with a special design. How about you?
3. High-quality items are often expensive. Low-cost items often break easily. Is there a way to buy low-cost, high-quality items?

17 Asian Cultures

Part 1: Tai Chi

Read the following article. Track 34

Tai chi is an ancient form of exercise. Millions of people practice it. Tai chi involves slow movements of the arms, legs, and body. Each movement exercises different muscles. The most common type of tai chi is the Yang style. It was developed 200 years ago.

Tai chi helps balance the body and mind. In this way, it makes them both strong. Tai chi looks easy to do, but it isn't. People practice for years to become good at it.

Vocabulary Check

Write the correct word in each blank.

common	balance	practice	muscles

1. Most people try to ____________ work and fun in their lives.
2. After such a long walk, all of my ____________ are tired.
3. The concert is next Friday. The band will ____________ every day until then.
4. Heavy traffic is a ____________ problem during rush hour.

Reading Check

Choose the best answer.

1. (   ) Tai chi is a(n) ____________ kind of exercise.
   A: unpopular   B: fast
   C: slow   D: modern

2. (   ) Tai chi is good for ____________.
   A: older people only
   B: just a few of the body's muscles
   C: people in very few countries
   D: the body and mind

3. (   ) What is the Yang style?
   A: A popular style of tai chi
   B: A movement
   C: A muscle
   D: A fighting contest

4. (   ) What does the article say about tai chi?
   A: It's impossible to teach.
   B: It takes time to learn to do tai chi well.
   C: Everybody is good at it.
   D: Most tai chi movements are for the arms.

Grammar Check

Write the correct word in each blank.

Ex: It feels good to take a shower after ___*exercising*___**.**
(exercised / exercising)

1. There are many ____________ ways to exercise.
   (different/ difference)

2. The book is very ____________.
   (interested/ interesting)

3. Do you like ____________ in Australia?
   (living/ live)

4. That ____________ is actually quite smart.
   (animal/ animals)

Part 2: Lucky Symbols of Chinese Culture

Read the following information.

In Chinese culture, there are a variety of lucky symbols. Many things can be lucky: animals, food, plants, colors, and so on. Here are a few, with the ways they are lucky:

Animals	
Fish	Making money
Bat	Good luck

Food	
Peach	Long life
Radish	Good luck

Objects	
Jade	Keeping safe
Old coins	Making money

True or False

Circle true (T) or false (F).

1. (T/F) Fish and old coins are lucky for making money.

2. (T/F) Jade is a symbol of long life.

3. (T/F) The article does not talk about lucky numbers.

4. (T/F) For good luck, hanging up a picture of a radish might help.

Dictation

A. Listen and fill in the blanks. Track 35

Hector: What do you have there, Jia-lin? I love the design and
1( ) colors.

Jia-lin: It's a Chinese character meaning "spring." We put it
2( ) during Chinese New Year, but in a special way.

Hector: How so?

Jia-lin: We turn it upside down. That means spring
3( ). Do you want to help me hang it?

Hector: Sure! How about right here?

Jia-lin: Perfect, thank you. Now we'll both have 4( )!

B. Choose the best answer.

1. ( ) Hector helps Jia-lin ______ the sign.
   A: hang B: design
   C: choose D: remove

2. ( ) What do we learn about the sign?
   A: There are two Chinese characters on it.
   B: The sign's colors are dark.
   C: Hector gave it to Jia-lin as a present.
   D: It brings people good luck.

Discussion

Discuss these questions together.

1. Do you do any exercise like tai chi or yoga? How about any martial arts like judo or karate?
2. What are some lucky symbols of your culture?
3. What's your favorite holiday? Do you do anything special at that time?

18 Modern Life

Part 1: A Hard but Happy Life

Read the following story. Track 36

Mr. Garcia works very hard. He wakes up every morning at 6:30 AM. One hour later, he takes the subway to his office. Everyone is so busy there. Sometimes, Mr. Garcia doesn't have time to eat lunch. The workday ends at 5:30 PM, but staying overtime is common.

Mr. Garcia is always happy to go home. He loves being with his family, talking with his wife, and playing with his children. Spending time with them makes him strong. He's ready for the next long day at the office.

Vocabulary Check

Write the correct word(s) in each blank.

wake up	overtime	children	family

1. What time did you ____________ today?
2. Mrs. Takara has three ____________: two girls and one boy.
3. Some of my ____________ members live in Singapore.
4. I can't go out tonight. I have to work ____________ again.

Reading Check

Choose the best answer.

1. (   ) Mr. Garcia ___________ every day.
   A: is at the office until 6:30 PM
   B: works about five hours
   C: takes a bus to his office
   D: goes to work at 7:30 AM

2. (   ) What do we learn about the people at Mr. Garcia's office?
   A: They take long breaks at 12:00.
   B: They rarely work overtime.
   C: They eat lunch together.
   D: They have a lot of work to do.

3. (   ) What words could describe Mr. Garcia?
   A: Angry and worried
   B: Unusual and curious
   C: Unhappy and tired
   D: Hard-working and busy

4. (   ) Which of the following is true?
   A: Mr. Garcia often works at home.
   B: Mr. Garcia doesn't have any children.
   C: Mr. Garcia enjoys being with his family.
   D: Mr. Garcia wants to change his life.

Grammar Check

Write the correct form of each verb.

Ex: Are they ___*leaving*___ **(leave) at 5:00 or 6:00?**

1. This morning, Dana will ___________ (start) work at 8:00.

2. She often ___________ (bake) cookies for friends.

3. What time does the train ___________ (arrive) at the station?

4. Are you ___________ (eat) dinner with us tonight?

Part 2: Daily Routine

Read the following information.

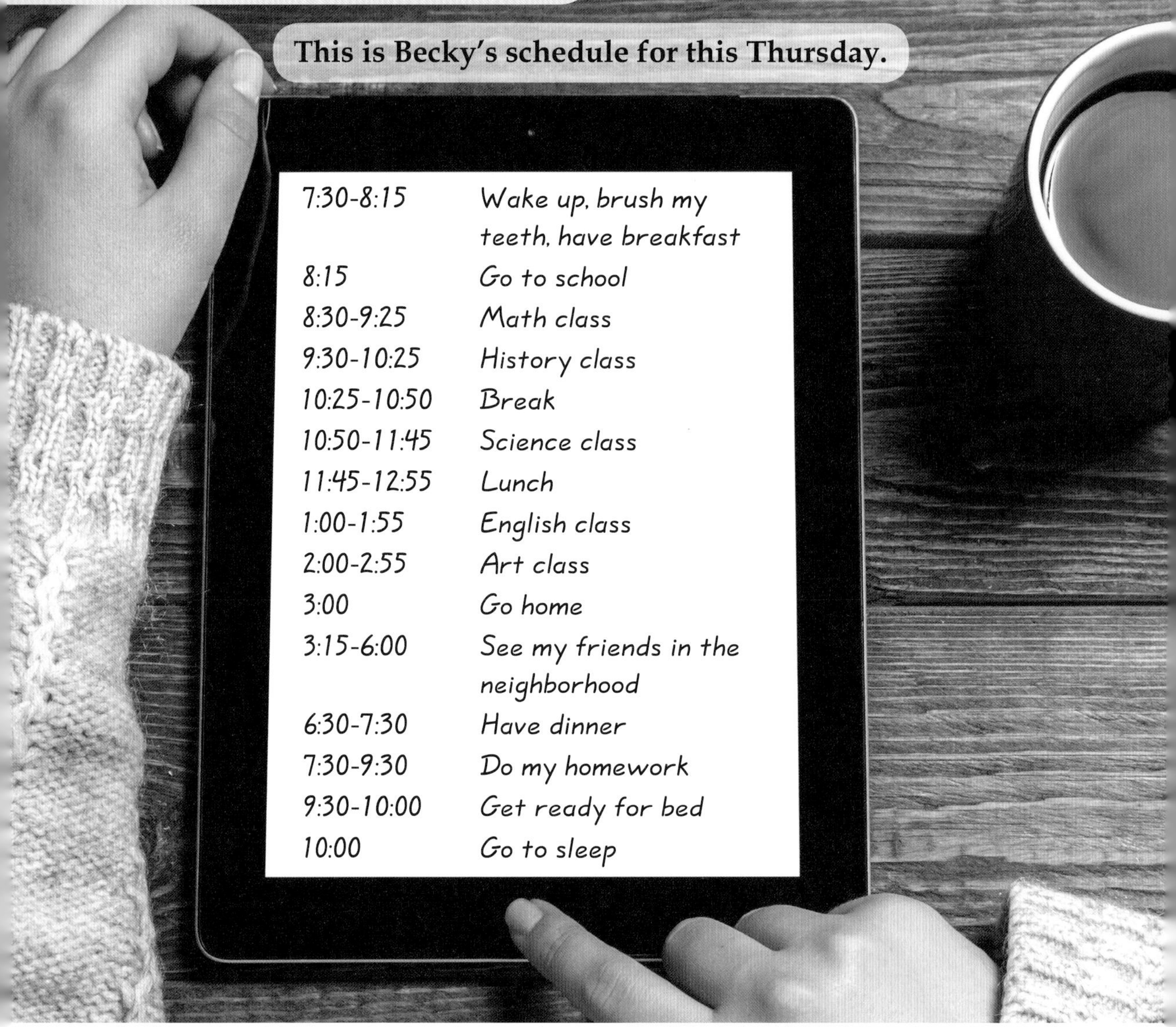

This is Becky's schedule for this Thursday.

7:30-8:15	Wake up, brush my teeth, have breakfast
8:15	Go to school
8:30-9:25	Math class
9:30-10:25	History class
10:25-10:50	Break
10:50-11:45	Science class
11:45-12:55	Lunch
1:00-1:55	English class
2:00-2:55	Art class
3:00	Go home
3:15-6:00	See my friends in the neighborhood
6:30-7:30	Have dinner
7:30-9:30	Do my homework
9:30-10:00	Get ready for bed
10:00	Go to sleep

True or False

Circle true (T) or false (F).

1. (T/F) On Thursday, Becky will wake up at 9:30 AM.

2. (T/F) She will see her neighborhood friends in the morning.

3. (T/F) In the afternoon, Becky will have two classes.

4. (T/F) She will do her homework before dinner.

Dictation

A. Listen and fill in the blanks. Track 37

Melanie: Long time, no see, Marco. How have you been?

Marco: Super busy. Last month, I joined the debate team. We practice 1(   ) a week.

Melanie: That's a lot. Are you still on the track team?

Marco: I sure am. We have a 2(   ) this Friday.

Melanie: Nice. You really have your hands full. 3(   ), I just watch my little brother.

Marco: That's important, too. Hey, do you guys want to come to the race?

Melanie: I'd love to! I'll talk to 4(   ).

B. Choose the best answer.

1. (   ) Why is Marco so busy?
   A: He has hard classes.
   B: He works three days a week.
   C: He is on two teams.
   D: He started racing last month.

2. (   ) What do we learn about Melanie?
   A: She is also on the debate team.
   B: She takes care of her sister.
   C: She isn't interested in seeing a race.
   D: She hasn't seen Marco recently.

Discussion

Discuss these questions together.

1. Do you have a busy schedule?
2. What do you do in your free time?
3. Some people want to work hard and make a lot of money. Others want to work less and have a simple life. How about you?

19 Growing Things

Part 1: Gardening

Read the following article. Track 38

To plant a garden, you only need a few things: tools, seeds, and soil. It's easy to grow many types of plants and flowers, such as roses and daisies. They all need water and light to grow, as well as daily attention. The size of a garden isn't important. It may be in a backyard on a large plot of land. Or it might be in a meter-long box inside a house.

Gardening helps people relax. It's also a wonderful feeling to take care of something and watch it grow. On top of that, a garden is a beautiful sight enjoyed by friends and relatives.

Vocabulary Check

Write the correct word in each blank.

grow	garden	wonderful	relatives

1. We have tulips and daisies in our ____________.

2. Your dog is huge. How did he ____________ so quickly?

3. On my mom's 60th birthday, 11 ____________ joined us for dinner.

4. You did a ____________ job with the salad. It's so good.

Reading Check

Choose the best answer.

1. (　　) Without water and light, ________.
   A: a garden only needs careful attention
   B: plants and flowers cannot grow
   C: people cannot buy seeds for a garden
   D: a garden needs to be large

2. (　　) The article mentions roses and daisies to ________.
   A: discuss the most popular flowers
   B: give examples of choices for a flower garden
   C: suggest the best flowers for a gift
   D: show the importance of bright colors in a garden

3. (　　) In the third sentence, "they" means ________.
   A: plants and flowers
   B: tools
   C: friends and relatives
   D: soil

4. (　　) Which benefit of gardening is not mentioned?
   A: Helping you relax
   B: Giving you a good feeling
   C: Growing food to eat
   D: Sharing something nice to look at

Grammar Check

Put the words in the correct order.

1. (to plant / this year / I / more orchids / want)

____.

2. (need / inside / we / the aloe plant / Do / to move)

____?

3. (take care of / garden / easy / a small / It's / to)

____.

Part 2: Growing Fruits and Vegetables

Read the following information.

Here are some tips and information for growing popular fruits and vegetables.

Fruit or Vegetable	Growing Tips	Best Planting Season
Broccoli	It does best when it's 20 degrees outside.	Early spring or late summer
Tomatoes	Water the plants often.	Early summer
Green Peppers	They love heat and sunshine.	Early summer
Spinach	Spinach plants need fresh air. Plants shouldn't be too close together.	Late summer
Strawberries	It's important to plant them at the right depth. They shouldn't be too deep in the soil.	Spring

True or False

Circle true (T) or false (F).

1. (T/F) It's best to plant tomatoes and green peppers in the spring.

2. (T/F) Strawberries should be planted at just the right depth.

3. (T/F) For broccoli, there are two good planting seasons.

4. (T/F) Make sure each row of spinach plants is crowded.

Dictation

A. Listen and fill in the blanks. Track 39

Itsuki: I love your garden! These lilies are incredible.

Kate: Thanks! My brother and I are in here working 1( ).

Itsuki: How did you learn so much?

Kate: Partly from our dad. He works at a gardening center. Sometimes he 2( ) seeds and plants.

Itsuki: Lucky for you. We have 3( ) at home. My favorite is our little cherry tomato plant.

Kate: Those are delicious. Do you want to trade 4( ) for some lilies?

Itsuki: All right!

B. Choose the best answer.

1. ( ) Kate gets new seeds from ___________.
   A: Itsuki B: her brother
   C: Itsuki's parents D: her father

2. ( ) What are Kate and Itsuki going to do next?
   A: Buy some plants
   B: Make a trade
   C: Start a new garden
   D: Eat dinner

Discussion

Discuss these questions together.

1. Do you have any plants or flowers in your home?
2. Have you ever planted your own fruits or vegetables? If not, would you like to try?
3. What are some good and bad points about having a garden?

20 Languages

Part 1: Sign Language

Read the following article. Track 40

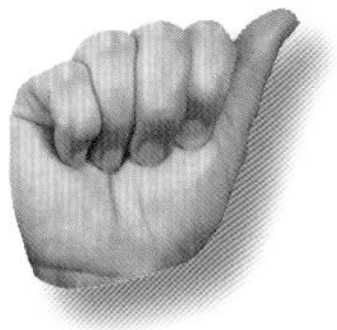

'A'

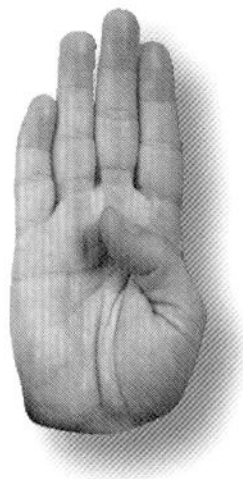

'B'

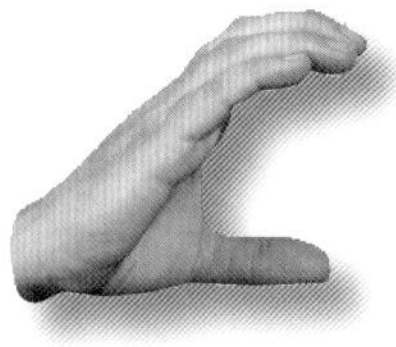

'C'

Deaf people use sign language to communicate with each other and with non-deaf people. There are hundreds of different sign languages worldwide. They are like spoken languages, with their own vocabulary words and grammar rules. Schools for the deaf use sign language in class.

Signs are made by making shapes with one's hands. A sign may include moving one's hands or pointing in a certain direction. For example, in American Sign Language, to say "smart," point to your forehead with your middle finger. In some languages, the expressions on a signer's face change the meaning of the sign.

Vocabulary Check

Write the correct word in each blank.

direction	shape	meaning	deaf

1. The bag is a strange ____________. It looks like a boat.
2. Walk 200 meters in that ____________. You'll see the train station.
3. I use sign language to communicate with my ____________ friend.
4. I don't understand the ____________ of that sentence.

Reading Check

Choose the best answer.

1. (   ) How are signs made?
   A: With a person's mouth
   B: With a person's eyes
   C: With a person's forehead
   D: With a person's hands

2. (   ) How are sign languages similar to spoken languages?
   A: They are both used to communicate with deaf people.
   B: They both have their own rules and vocabulary words.
   C: They both have exactly the same kinds of grammar.
   D: They are both used in every school around the world.

3. (   ) What is another way to say "for example"?
   A: for instance
   B: in that
   C: in such a way
   D: all along

4. (   ) Why are a person's expressions important in some sign languages?
   A: They can change a person's face.
   B: They can change the shape of a person's hands.
   C: They can change a sign's meaning.
   D: They can change the grammar of the language.

Grammar Check

Complete each sentence with *to*, *of*, or *for*.

Ex: The camera is designed ___*to*___ take photos underwater.

1. There were thousands __________ fans at the concert.

2. I bought this shirt __________ you in Vietnam.

3. This is the sign used __________ say "hello."

4. I didn't understand the meaning __________ the poem.

Part 2: Learning English

Read the following conversation.

Teo: What's your favorite class? Mine's math.

Rosa: English, for sure.

Teo: Why is that?

Rosa: It's fun to speak a second language. I feel like a different person.

Teo: That's interesting. But what about the homework? It's so hard.

Rosa: Every class has homework, right?

Teo: That's true. Hey, do you want to study together for next week's test?

Rosa: Sure. Two heads are better than one.

True or False

Circle true (T) or false (F).

1. (T/F) The friends have different favorite classes.

2. (T/F) Rosa finds learning English interesting.

3. (T/F) Teo thinks the English class has easy homework.

4. (T/F) Rosa says, "Two heads are better than one." She means working with someone makes things easier.

Dictation

A. Listen and fill in the blanks. Track 41

Emika: I love old 1(   ) movies. They're so dramatic.

Jerry: Do you have any favorites?

Emika: Anything with Humphrey Bogart. I sometimes watch with the English subtitles on. I can learn 2(   ) and phrases that way.

Jerry: Good idea. But aren't some phrases 3(   ) old-fashioned?

Emika: Some are. I like watching new movies, too. It's fun to see how English has changed 4(   ).

Jerry: Wow, soon you'll be a movie expert and an English expert!

B. Choose the best answer.

1. (   ) To improve her English, Emika ___________.
   A: visits a website about actors   B: turns on movie subtitles
   C: talks to a movie expert   D: reads phrase books

2. (   ) What does Jerry suggest about old movies?
   A: They are usually less dramatic than new movies.
   B: They may use phrases that aren't common anymore.
   C: They are interesting because they are black and white.
   D: They can only be understood by movie experts.

Discussion

Discuss these questions together.

1. In the future, how will you probably use English? (Ex: for work, for travel)
2. Do you ever watch old movies or listen to old music? If so, have you learned any English that way?
3. What are some fun ways to improve one's English?

Reading Links 2 [B-923]

リーディング・リンクス 2

1 刷	2021 年 1 月 18 日
2 刷	2023 年 3 月 31 日
著 者	アンドルー E. ベネット Andrew E. Bennett
発行者	南雲 一範 Kazunori Nagumo
発行所	株式会社 南雲堂 〒162-0801 東京都新宿区山吹町 361 NAN' UN-DO CO.,Ltd. 361 Yamabuki-cho, Shinjuku-ku, Tokyo 162-0801, Japan 振替口座：00160-0-46863 TEL：03-3268-2311(代表) ／ FAX：03-3269-2486
編集者	加藤 敦
製 版	Andrew E. Bennett
装 丁	銀月堂
検 印	省略
コード	ISBN 978-4-523-17923-8 C0082

Printed in Japan

E-mail nanundo@post.email.ne.jp
URL http://www.nanun-do.co.jp/